Desire and Imitation
in International Politics

STUDIES IN VIOLENCE, MIMESIS, AND CULTURE

Desire and Imitation in International Politics

Jodok Troy

Michigan State University Press · *East Lansing*

♾ The paper used in this publication meets the minimum requirements
of ANSI/NISO Z39.48-1992 (R 1997) (Permanence of Paper).

Michigan State University Press
East Lansing, Michigan 48823-5245

LIBRARY OF CONGRESS CATALOGING-IN-PUBLICATION DATA
Names: Troy, Jodok, author.
Title: Desire and imitation in international politics / Jodok Troy.
Description: East Lansing : Michigan State University Press, [2021]
| Series: Studies in violence, mimesis, and culture
| Includes bibliographical references and index.
Identifiers: LCCN 2020020755 | ISBN 9781611863888 (paperback)
| ISBN 9781609176624 | ISBN 9781628954210 | ISBN 9781628964226
Subjects: LCSH: International relations—Social aspects.
| Conflict management—Political aspects.
| Desire (Philosophy)—Political aspects. | Imitation—Political aspects.
Classification: LCC JZ1251 .T76 2021 | DDC 327.1—dc23
LC record available at https://lccn.loc.gov/2020020755

Book design by Charlie Sharp, Sharp Des!gns, East Lansing, Michigan
Cover design by David Drummond, Salamander Design, www.salamanderhill.com.
Cover art is *The Music Room* (1907), by Vilhelm Hammershoi (1864–1916),
71.9 × 58.9 cms. Used with permission of Bridgeman Images.

Michigan State University Press is a member of the Green Press Initiative and is
committed to developing and encouraging ecologically responsible publishing
practices. For more information about the Green Press Initiative and the use
of recycled paper in book publishing, please visit *www.greenpressinitiative.org.*

Visit Michigan State University Press at *www.msupress.org*

For my family.

Contents

Foreword

Richard Ned Lebow

Realists believe that international relations are all about security and that we would have a peaceful world if the status quo powers had unquestioned military superiority and the resolve to use it in defense of the international order. Liberals believe that politics, domestic and international, are all about possessions and that we would have a peaceful world if everyone had enough material goods. Theorists in both paradigms assume that political actors are largely rational and define rationality in a manner consonant with their claims. Their formulations verge on the tautological: Realists define rational in international relations as the pursuit of security, and liberals as the pursuit of wealth.

Their logical contradictions aside, both paradigms err in more fundamental ways. They are based on unduly restrictive assumptions about human motivation. Fearful people may put their security above other considerations, but it flies in the face of reality to think that most peoples and states feel threatened most of the time by other states. If people in the great powers are threatened, it is increasingly by nonstate actors, pathogens, terrorists—most of whom are homegrown—and the consequences of neoliberalism and globalization. Military force has marginal utility at best in coping with these problems. The same is true of wealth. People want material possessions, but they also want respect, sympathy, affection, sex, good health, attractive bodies, education, and any number of other things. The World Values Survey indicates that after people achieve a moderate degree of economic security, they opt for increases in status over increases in wealth.[1]

Modern theories of politics and international relations have all but excluded the quest for honor, standing, and status. They are nevertheless very much present in political life, and I tried to bring them into the picture in *A Cultural Theory of International Relations*.[2] In a follow-up book, I assembled a data set of all wars fought since 1648 that had at least one rising or great power on each side. Among other things I coded for was initiator motives for going to war. Over 60 percent of leaders were motivated by the quest for honor or standing or by revenge, the latter as a result of losing status in a previous violent conflict. This percentage does not decline over the centuries.[3]

I do not believe that any one motive should be given precedent over others. For this reason, most paradigms and theories in international relations that do show a poor fit with reality. For most people, and that includes political actors, multiple motives are in play most of the time. Social scientists must identify the diversity of motives, the contexts in which they are likely to be paramount, and the ways in which they influence thinking and behavior. International relations is a subset of human behavior, and fewer motives and emotions may be in play, but they are still plentiful. To cite just a few examples, Irving Janis and Leon Mann have made a case for anxiety reduction; Avner Offer and I among others, for honor; and Felix Berenskoetter for friendship.[4]

Our goals and behavior are very much influenced by our peer group and the wider society. Constructivists argue that society constitutes us and provides roles. In a more general sense, it teaches us who we are, what we should aspire to be, and how it is to be achieved. International practice is rooted in a normative order.[5] States function in a society, not in a system, as Realists would have it, and their leaders are generally very responsive to cues from other actors. In all societies, actors seek recognition, a key means of enhancing self-esteem. Actors' goals and behavior are shaped by what peer groups and societies define as admirable.

What is valued changes over time. In international society, status was formerly attained through slashing, burning, and territorial expansion. Today, war and conquest are frowned upon, and states that draw the sword without authorization from appropriate international organizations lose standing, as the United States and Russia have in recent years. Contemporary states achieve status in diverse ways: through political and economic innovation and leadership, wealth, looking after their citizens, foreign aid and humanitarian assistance, providing common goods, and cultural, scientific, and sporting achievements. There is an ongoing struggle not only for status but over the nature of the status hierarchy. Leaders want their state's pathway to status to be highly valued. Where you stand depends entirely on the judgments of others. States, like people, accordingly have strong incentives to impress foreign leaders and publics in favorable ways and to convince others, but example or pressure, to emulate them. International relations, like social relations, involve role models and imitation. People and states are constantly comparing themselves to others, and mimicking or distancing themselves depending on their judgments about which will enhance their status. Because Louis XIV, at the apex of the status hierarchy, built palaces and gardens and supported the arts and sciences, other rulers aped him, and in the process confirmed the French king's status. The same would hold true of colonies, navies, nuclear weapons, and space exploration.

This is where Jodok Troy enters the picture. Drawing on mimetic theory, he explores why people and states practice imitation. Mimetic theory assumes that human beings are driven to behave this way and that it is a source of conflict. When everybody wants the same thing and there is only so much of it to go around, competition and conflict are inevitable. What is important here is the arrow of influence. It is not scarcity that causes conflict but common, if not universal, desires for something that is responsible for scarcity. It is a social construction not a material condition. This insight has all kinds of important implications for international relations, and this book does an excellent job of teasing them out.

Mimetic theory extends the boundaries of international relations to the social world because this is the source of much imitation. Epistemologically, it makes no sense to pretend that international relations—or economics, for that matter—are separate, largely self-contained domains that can be studied on their basis of their own internal dynamics. Troy contends that Hans Morgenthau understood this fundamental truth about politics, but this aspect of his thinking had received little to no attention. Mimetic theory helps to bring out the intersubjective and relational features of classical Realism and of the practice of international relations. It offers insight into power and its changing nature. Of equal interest, it allows a novel exploration of the evolving relationship between the sacred and the profane and their implications for international cooperation and conflict.

Troy's book meets a high standard for intellectual innovation, thoughtful analysis, and careful empirical work. It speaks to diverse communities: constructivists, Realists, humanists, and even policymakers. I have learned much from reading it.

Preface

arry S. Truman, former president of the United States, believed that politics and social life is about "competition without shooting each other."[1] He assumed that humans are competitive rather than aggressive.[2] Indeed, humans constantly compete with their peers in private life, at work, and certainly in politics. According to mimetic theory, this is because they compete in imitating the desire of others ("mimesis"). Studies in identity politics come to the same conclusion.[3] At the same time, humans struggle to make themselves distinct to point to the differences between themselves and others. In a world that increasingly grows together, this is an important individual asset. It is therefore sameness, not difference, that turns out to be at the root of many social and political problems.[4]

Mimetic theory assumes that the fundamental drive of human conduct is the imitation of the desire of others.[5] Humans do not know what to choose for themselves and thus imitate what others desire. Gilbert Keith Chesterton aptly formulated a critique of this all too human desire:

> In the modern ideal conceptions of society there are some desires that are possibly not attainable: but there are some desires that are not desirable. That men should live in equally beautiful houses is a dream that may or

may not be attained. But that all men should live in the same beautiful
house is not a dream at all; it is a nightmare.[6]

Humans do not only fight over differences. Rather, human conduct is potentially conflictual because humans are the same and imitate the desires of
others, which leads to endless competition among humans. Eventually, the
scapegoat mechanism, the persecution of a victim, solves the mimetic crisis.
Sacrificial rituals are a common form to canalize violence, which often led
to the founding of religions and cultures.[7] Although analyses of domestic
political problems pick up this train of thought, it is less recognized in the
international realm.[8] There, the continuing existence and bloody outcomes
of international events, recurring patterns of power-seeking political actors,
revolutions, or the prevailing occurrence of violence within societies puzzle
International Relations. Much of the lack of comprehension traces back
to a one-sided view that is stuck in the assumption that if valued goods
were only equally distributed, peace would prevail. Peace, in other words,
is assumed to be a status conditioned upon the satisfaction and rational
distribution of certain goods.[9] Still, we have "All these theories yet the bodies keep piling up."[10]

International Relations and international political theory, I argue in
this book, fail to acknowledge what mimetic theory is aware of and what
classical Realism hinted to during the foundational years of the discipline in
the twentieth century: human conduct and thus politics cannot avoid the
desire for power. The imitation of desire of others is the cause of many of
international politics' most persistent problems. It is not only a scarcity of
and the missing distribution of resources that drive rivalry. Rather, it is often
the other way around. Research on revolutions and identity politics reinforce
the theoretical claims of mimetic theory. Relative deprivation drives the "gap
between what people feel rightfully entitled to and what they are capable
of achieving under existing circumstances."[11] Among others, the continuing
existence of nationalism, political religion, intra group violence, longing for
nuclear weapons, diplomatic aspirations of non-state actors, and societal
changes are outcomes beyond actors' will only to survive.

Mimetic theory gained some resonance in International Relations
research but struggles to gain traction.[12] This is not surprising. Mimetic
theory challenges some of the discipline's core assumptions such as the

autonomy of the individual, violence as a subordinate of politics, a clear-cut distinction between the religious and secular realm, and the assumption of (a liberal) order as the default status in political conduct. International Relations assumes that faults in international political conduct can be fixed if the appropriate instruments are applied.[13] Conducting research this way, International Relations misses that actors imitate the desire of others, that they are not as autonomous as the International Relations canon holds, and that those patterns affect international politics because the success of instruments (e.g., the human rights regime) and values (e.g., democracy) is measured at the standards of others.[14] In other words, rationalism, as described by Michael Oakshott, dominates current International Relations' theory and much of its practice:

> the conduct of affairs for the rationalist is a matter of solving problems . . . the politics it inspires may be called the politics of the felt need . . . political life is resolved into a series of crises each to be surmounted by the application of "reason" . . . (rationalist politics) are the politics of perfection and they are the politics of uniformity . . . the rationalist cannot imagine a politics that does not consist of solving problems or a political problem of which there is no rational solution . . . (and while) there may not be one universal remedy for all political ills . . . the remedy for any particular ill is as universal in its application as it is rational in its conception.[15]

Prominent Realist scholars such as Hans J. Morgenthau have been aware of the problems that scholars of mimetic theory like René Girard and critics of rationalism like Oakshott point out. However, those insights are either forgotten, ignored, assumed as not important, or have simply not been discovered yet. Mimetic theory and critics of rationalism point out that at the roots of this rationalist take on theory and practice lies a certain doctrine of human knowledge. The classical approach's take on political "practice" illustrates that this doctrine confuses the requirements of practice, technical knowledge, and practical knowledge. Technical knowledge is the knowledge of "rules which are, or may be, deliberately learned, remembered and . . . put into practice." Practical knowledge is knowledge that "exists only in use, is not reflective and [unlike technique] cannot be formulated into rules'. In rationalism these two are collapsed into one: technical knowledge."[16]

In this book, I attempt to bring together Morgenthau's Realism and Girard's mimetic theory to see what a marriage of convenience could look like and what they could achieve together in better understanding international politics. I take a critical stance on modern-day political science and International Relations and their quest to solve puzzles as if all political problems are accessible to rationalist frameworks and solutions. "Were it not for ignorance and emotions," Morgenthau argues, "reason would solve international conflicts as easily as and as rationally as it has solved so many problems in the field of the natural sciences."[17] In a certain way, Realism and mimetic theory are puzzle-solvers as well because they show us ways to approach the greatest puzzle of all—how to think about politics.

Seen from this angle, the book is a nomothetic attempt, which will give rise to criticism. The "disenchanted" world, to use Max Weber's term, has become more complex, not simpler. Frequently, and legitimately so, International Relations counters this complexity with ideographic explanations based on single case studies, testing theories and hypotheses. However, as I attempt to illustrate in this book, "without the ability to think symbolically, we find it harder to navigate the world, not easier. Why? Because the symbolic allows for mystery and uncertainty, which (if you haven't noticed) is what most of our human experience is comprised of."[18] Equally, this narrative and novelistic approach holds valuable insights on the intellectual history of Morgenthau and others' Realism, whose arguments, according to Martti Koskenniemi,

> led beyond law as the banal application of (formal) rules but also beyond sociology and ethics as scientific disciplines or bureaucratic techniques. Instead, they brought into existence international relations as an academic discipline that would deal "realistically" with the functioning of eternal human laws in a condition of anarchy. Already the problem-setting involved a contradiction. Realism claimed to be based on science; yet its argument was anti-scientific. The "eternal laws" of politics claimed the status of deep insights tint social and psychological life. But the polemics against the behavioralists had been directed precisely against the idea that the field could be reduced to scientific laws.[19]

Discovering Realism and Mimetic Theory

I do not seek to look into Girard and his take on mimetic theory as another thinker and to normalize that thinker for International Relations. Nor do I set out to call for a "mimetic turn" in International Relations. Rather, I aim to point out, first, that International Relations' analysis can gain a supplemental conceptual perspective by discovering insights from mimetic theory. Second, toward this end, I discover rather than confirm some of the basic commitments and epistemological assumptions of classical Realism with the help of mimetic theory.[20]

While I focus on Realism in terms of Morgenthau, I also look at the broader Realist tradition. It is the focus on and concept of practice that makes the classical approach a valuable guide to focus on mimetic desire and how it influences agency and practice in international politics.[21] The classical approach rests on what Martin Hollis and Steve Smith declared as the insider account of studying politics.[22] Other than the outsider (spectator) approach of the natural science tradition, which stresses the explanation to identify laws of the social and political realm, the insider approach stresses interpretation. The inside approach in particular "is to learn to make sense of and to perform actions, taking place *inside* the contexts of distinctive practices. There is no external, social scientific way of learning such practice-dependent performances."[23] Such an approach helps International Relations research conduct to gain deeper insights into the impacts of mimetic desire as it looks at the intentions of actor's conduct rather than the causes of actor's behavior. Mimetic desire is an essential and functional component of the action that "takes place among entities, rather than being generated by them."[24]

Like Hedley Bull, I take the international as a generalized one, acknowledging the general uncertainty of a "sphere where security and order are not the ultimate aim, but where complexity and diversity are acknowledged and dealt with politically, not obliterated."[25] Many of International Relations' theoretical shortcomings addressing this concept of the international trace back to the premises of Realism, much of which mimetic theory shares, particularly an anti-rationalist point of view on the conduct of politics. Moreover, Realism and mimetic theory's epistemology start from assumptions of violence and disorder. They acknowledge that throughout history, violence has been a persistent feature of human conduct and war has been the basis of legal and social structures.[26] Mimetic theory digs even deeper into the epistemology, ontology, and teleology of international politics. Only a few scholars deal with mimetic theory, and even fewer discuss the International Relations canon against the foil of mimetic theory. After all, as signaled earlier, mimetic theory illuminates as well as challenges the substantial aspects of the international in terms of the social, sacred, and global facets.[27]

Realism, as I take it here, frames politics and power as intersubjective and relational concepts.[28] Not surprisingly, then, these assumptions determine large parts of Realism's methodological approach. Realism, while having a keen eye on agency, points to the political and power as intersubjective and relational concepts. Like mimetic theory, it approaches societal aspects of international politics under the assumption of violence and disorder as the principal social condition. However, Realism holds that power evolves from dialogue between actors. Hence, the classical approaches of Realism and the English School are intriguing as a methodological lens. These approaches take practice as constitutive of international politics bound by the struggle for power that evolved rather than being something intentionally generated by the actors. On the other side, the explanation of violence that mimetic theory offers is foremost processual rather than substantial. However, International Relations also needs a debate, as Friedrich Kratochwil suggests, based on "a closer engagement with the *substantive issues characterizing political action*, and the realm of praxis."[29] In the course of this book, I illustrate that mimetic theory also provides insights into substantial aspects of international politics.

At the example of nationalism, Faared Zakaria points out one of today's major paradoxes: "desire for recognition and respect is surging throughout the world. It may seem paradoxical that globalization and economic modernization are breeding political nationalism. But that is only if we view nationalism as a backward ideology, certain to be erased by the onward march of progress."[30] I illustrate that the desire for power is the desire for recognition. Other than liberal and critical approaches of International Relations, mimetic theory and Realism point to the dangers of a rising global culture that is prone to generate rivalry, competition, and thus more conflict.[31] Mimetic theory, then, provides insights into the interplay of the evolving and nature of power. This is obvious at the example of one of mimetic theory's most plain postulates regarding human conduct: sameness is the agitator and troublemaker in the social sphere, not difference.[32]

Mimetic theory, then, also challenges the prevailing liberal notion of a clear-cut distinction between a secular political and a sacred religious sphere.[33] Religion and religious violence are thriving topics of today's International Relations research. Mimetic theory is mainly a theory about the origins of culture and religion. Not surprisingly, the bulk of International Relations studies turning to mimetic theory thus is interested in issues of religion and violence.[34] Mimetic theory can indeed contribute theorizing on religious issues in international politics. For example, the "global resurgence of religion" proves the secularization thesis wrong—contending that modernization leads to decline of religion or at least to its privatization.[35] Religion is in the focus of International Relations academia, "God is back," and the discipline seems to have come to terms with religion.[36] However, existing International Relations' research does so by recognizing specific actors and less so by a substantive engagement with the relational features and even constitutive entanglement between the religious sphere and the political sphere.[37]

Compared to existing International Relations literature dealing with mimetic theory and religion, I point out that Realism is prone to follow up on mimetic theory's assumption of the linkage between sacred violence and secular political order. This kinship between mimetic theory and classical Realism partly exists because Realism itself developed out of a critique of secularism.[38] Research on mimetic theory and conflict routinely points out the dangers of imitation and desire and the destructive forces of human character traits at great length.[39] In parts, I do as well. However, a conceptual engagement with mimetic theory within the field of International Relations also brings to light rather positive outcomes.[40] Being aware of the implications of mimetic theory's and Realism's insights into the darkness and destructive facets of human conduct is the first step to overcome them. While mimetic desire might be responsible for many violent acts, mimetic desire, as Girard himself is keen to point out, is "intrinsically good."[41]

Mimetic theory is certainly in danger of being overstretched and oversimplified. It can be overstretched when used for every phenomenon that comes along in international politics. It can be oversimplified, for example, by using the scapegoat mechanism as an excuse for explaining certain policies. Considering that the scapegoat mechanism, in terms of Girard's theory, only works if perpetrators are convinced of the guilt of the victim, it is obvious that it is first an anthropological theory. Adapting anthropological theories may prove to be too limiting to explain every political action. In particular, psychological and socio-psychological studies show potential for explaining issues such as perception and misperception closely related to mimetic theory's explanatory potential.[42]

As Morgenthau's Realism stresses, "Politics is a struggle for power over men, and whatever its ultimate aim may be, power is its immediate goal and the modes of acquiring, maintaining, and demonstrating it determine the technique of political action."[43] In the words of Clifford Geertz, "The extraordinary has not gone out of modern politics, however much the banal may have entered; power not only still intoxicates, it still exalts."[44] It is therefore that politics, and even more so international politics, always have a tragic component hardwired into their conduct, affecting the epistemological and ontological conditions of politics and political practice.[45] Political action is inherently contradictory, pending between self-constitution and meaning. Much of rationalist social science analyses thus fall short to grasp the complexity of human nature.[46] For Realism, the concepts of the political and of power are relational ones, yet Realists are rather silent about the relational nature of actual political practices. The English School's notion of practice, as introduced in the next chapter, is therefore helpful. Similar to mimetic theory, it holds that particular actions, not only the concepts such as the political and power, take "place among entities, rather than being generated by them."[47]

Acknowledgments

This book is a result of the three-year stand-alone research project *Which Structure, Whose Virtue? Realism's Premises on Men and Power* (Austrian Science Fund, FWF project P 25198-G16). Although challenging in many ways, this project provided the opportunity for research and writing for which I am truly thankful. This book is also the result of many discussions with scholars around the globe who took an interest in the topics of the book. Several scholars and practitioners of international politics, the main protagonists of this book, may be long since dead but many colleagues helped me gain insights into their lives' work.

I sincerely want to thank the many colleagues who provided feedback on earlier versions of the manuscript. Although there is no way of naming them all, I want to thank Scott Thomas for continuing to encourage me in my studies on mimetic theory and International Relations; Wolfgang Palaver for his openness toward political science's perspective on religion and his enduring support; Christoph Frei for sharing and discussing insights on Hans Morgenthau; Christoph Rohde for his interests in matters of classical Realism; Robert Joustra for comments on early ideas of the manuscript; Alison McQueen for sharing interests in political theory; Ned Lebow for contributing the foreword; and the anonymous reviewers for providing feedback on earlier versions of the manuscript.

Parts of some chapters appeared previously as journal articles. I would like to thank the publishers Brill, SAGE, and Taylor & Francis for granting the permission to reuse them.

- "Faith-Based Diplomacy under Examination," *The Hague Journal of Diplomacy* 3, no. 3 (2008): 209-31.
- "Desire for Power or the Power of Desire? Mimetic Theory and the Heart of Twentieth-Century Realism," *Journal of International Political Theory* 11, no. 1 (2015): 26–41. Reprinted by permission of SAGE Publications.
- "Dag Hammarskjöld: An International Civil Servant Uniting Mystics and Realistic Diplomatic Engagement," *Diplomacy & Statecraft* 21, no. 3 (2010): 434-50, doi: 10.1080/09592296.2010.508414. Taylor & Francis, https://www.tandfonline.
- "The Power of the Political in an Urbanizing International," *Alternatives* 42, no. 4 (2017): 211–26. Reprinted by permission of SAGE Publications.

I would like to thank William Johnsen, Julie Loehr and Anastasia Wraight from Michigan State University Press for their careful attending to the manuscript all the way through publication. The usual disclaimers apply.

International Politics and Realist Thought

This book is not an attempt to rescue Realism from twisting its intellectual heritage with the help of mimetic theory.[1] Least of all do I claim that my reading of the Realist tradition is the accurate one. My aim is more modest. I turn to thinkers such as Hans Morgenthau in order to use their concepts and theoretical frameworks to understand various aspects of international political conduct. Introducing mimetic theory to such a project illustrates the explanatory and normative power of Realism, sheds light on epistemological issues with which Realism struggles, and discovers new facets in the bulk of Realist thought. This is in particular as mimetic theory is "a parsimonious, critical yet foundational, anti-rationalist, and intersubjective account to international politics that starts from the study of violence and ends with eschatology of salvation."[2] Mimetic theory, Realism and, to a lesser degree, the English School, which I take as an research enterprise closely related to Realism, share a wide array of epistemological assumptions. I take Realism as an approach relying on a distinct concept of power and politics. More specifically, as Alison McQueen proposes, Realism is

> a distinctive family of approaches to the study, practice, and normative
> evaluation of politics that tend to (a) affirm the autonomy (or, more

minimally, the distinctiveness) and contextual specificity of politics; (b) take disagreement, conflict, and power to be ineradicable and constitutive features of politics; (c) reject as "utopian," "idealist," or "moralist," those approaches, practices, and evaluations which seem to deny these facts; and (d) prioritise the requirements of political order and stability over the demands of justice (or, more minimally, reject the absolute priority of justice over other political values).[3]

The English School, on the other side, is an approach that primarily rests on the concept of international society, which is

> conceived as of a now-global society in which states are the primary actors, collectively producing the rules and accepted practices by which they manage their interrelations. The ES [English School] is a social theoretic approach in the sense, in which action reflects the ideas, cultural contexts, identities, and shared understandings of individual and state actors.[4]

The proposed framework and its subsequent qualitative methodology assumes that International Relations does not merely need more and better facts. In today's world the social sciences, and International Relations in particular, probably have as many facts and data available as ever before. Instead, I stress the need for supplementary ways of approaching the facts and data available, of looking how puzzle pieces fit together without perceiving International Relations genuinely as a rationalistic problem-solving science as pointed out earlier. This calls for a critical engagement with theory, questioning existing structures and orders, and going beyond a mere problem-solving approach of research puzzles in International Relations.[5] The Realist tradition, just like Isaiah Berlin and others emphasized, is keen not "to mistake increases in methodological precision for increases in genuine understanding."[6]

Such a nomothetic approach to theory does not immediately produce general propositions.[7] However, there is no view from nowhere. Reality is always interpreted reality.[8] Hence, I rely on an interpretive approach of epistemology and research design, based on the assumption that "people act on their beliefs and preferences" and that "we cannot read off people's beliefs and preferences from objective facts about them."[9] Paying attention to agency

and practice, a humanistic view of politics bridges interpretive and herme-
neutic approaches and normative theorizing. Such a view does not necessary
lead to humanistic answers but illustrates "what individual willpower can
do in foreign policy."[10] Yet international politics is not only about "human
conduct in a world of states," but also about human conduct in a world of
social and socialized actors and the relationships between them.[11] In other
words, relational "subjects are not related to each other in the weak sense of
being only empirically contiguous; they are ontologically related such that an
identity can only be deciphered by virtue of its 'place' in relationship to other
identities in its web."[12] Yet an interpretative approach is not to be confused
with *explaining* human conduct. In the classical approach,

> Interpreting human conduct does not involve discovering "true" motives
> or "real" intentions, and it does not involve explaining processes or forces
> that bring a particular state of affairs into being. The character of human
> conduct is disclosed, not in an unbroken chain of causes and effects, but in
> a particular context of activity; a context that conceives conduct "as actions
> and utterance, wise or foolish, which have reasons, adequate or inadequate,
> but not causes."[13]

In *National Interests in International Society*, Martha Finnemore points
toward actors encompassing their interests influenced by socialization.[14]
Norms and rules construct interests via the actors' understanding of the
social structure they find themselves confronted with. Interaction, then, constructs interests and identities. Ideas do matter for the Realist tradition but
they matter beyond instrumental constructs, as a rational framework tends
to frame them. It is not that mainstream International Relations sweeps
aside ideas. However, rationalist frameworks often treat them as constructs
to achieve certain ends.[15] I challenge this notion of norms and ideas and their
influence on international politics. In the next step, I delineate how Realism
understands practice and how this understanding challenges the positivist
notion of cause and effect of norms and ideas. One way to illustrate this is to
have a closer look at narrative theory.

In his narrative theory, Alasdair MacIntyre cautions not to separate
(subjective) ideas from their rationality and tradition (i.e., the objective context).[16] The implications of this caution become, for example, eminent in the

case of researching issues of religion and terrorism, where research tends to see the religious motivation out of context. "It is very difficult to understand terrorism or other forms of collective violence apart from how the people themselves involved understand their goals, values, and passions. It matters that terrorist groups or political movements are religious organizations, or are motivated by how they understand their religion."[17] Throughout the following chapters, this book evaluates the interplay between idea people, behavioral people, and relational people, as Charles Tilly framed them regarding the study of violence. Idea people stress that the basis of human conduct is consciousness, which shapes their conduct by ideas. Behavioral people stress the importance of the autonomy of motives, impulses, and opportunities. Relational people stress the importance of shaping personalities via the interaction and interchanges with others.[18]

In International Relations scholarship, Realism displays this aspect of focusing on Tilly's relational people. In its methodology, Realism is situated between interpretative approaches as outlined earlier (and opposed to approaches of explaining) without proposing law-like patterns of politics. Such an approach does not separate normative reasoning from an empirical understanding of political and social practices.[19] In other words, MacIntyre's and Tilly's approaches question a clear-cut distinction between facts and values, let alone that we can distinguish between the different purposes of knowledge claims.[20] It is one of the basic scientific premises of Realism that *how* political actors are doing things is at least as important as *what* they do. Hence, Morgenthau warns, "No study of politics and certainly no study of international politics in the mid-twentieth century can be disinterested in the sense that it is able to divorce knowledge from action and to pursue knowledge for its own sake."[21]

The research conduct of this book relies on qualitative and comparative methods in line with Realism's research agenda, which prefers a conceptual analysis, focusing on agents, agency, and ideal types. This analysis calls for and constructs a theoretical framework to interpret and "interrogate the practice of statespersons to discern its normative content" that are "constitutive of international order."[22] In the words of Martin Wight, International Relations "assumes that moral standards can be upheld without the heavens falling. And it assumes that the fabric of social and political life will be maintained, without accepting the doctrine that to preserve it any measures are permissible. For it assumes that the upholding of moral standards will in itself tend to strengthen the fabric of political life."[23]

Agents, Practice and Desire

The focus on agents, agency, and practice in international politics sets out from the aspiration to gain insights into its rules of conduct, which constitute a set of social relations, in other words, an institution. I rely on Jönsson and Hall's definition of an institution that takes it, broadly understood, "as a relatively stable collection of social practices consisting of easily recognized *roles* coupled with underlying *norms* and a set of *rules* or conventions defining appropriate behavior for, and governing relations among, occupants of these roles."[24] The rules of conduct that eventually constitute an institution in compliance with norms and practices do not cause anything by themselves. They "do not exist before being demonstrated in action."[25] They are effects, not causes as the positivist branch of research on international norms assumes. How international society and order is constructed and achieved is a question of the practice of the codes and rules of conduct of the participating actors in society. As a theory relying on philosophical and historical reflections on politics, Realism thus emphasizes practice and the local context of practice as the shaping condition of politics.[26]

International political practices, according to Chris Brown, are "understood as produced by inarticulate, practical, common-sense knowledge rather than by the application of theoretical knowledge."[27] This conception of practice emphasizes practices' telic notion: "A person engaging in a telic practice is *guided* by its standards rather than being *caused* to perform in some manner, and telic practices are directly accessible to empirical investigation."[28] For research conduct this means to study a wide range of contemporary and historical accounts and discover conceptual cores of the actions and practices of the objects under scrutiny together with the study of secondary literature in which the effects of the agent's actions have been set out.[29] A practice is a set of standards that do not cause something but guide the practitioner. It "is an activity—a form of action. It is 'socially established'—it is a social artefact. And it is marked by 'standards of excellence'—standards which define the activity."[30] It is thus that Martin Wight argued that the practice of diplomacy is based on the "requirements of social existence and true to the constant experience of diplomatic life."[31]

This understanding of practice opens up avenues of understanding mimesis's impact on international political conduct. However, not all international activity conforms to a practice. Fieldwork starts from the assumption that "contingency, habit and instrumental behaviour that ignores procedural constraints all fall outside an empirical understanding of practice."[32] Practices such as diplomacy are conducted according to standards of excellences, which are set forth in particular forms of interpretation.[33] It is therefore that there can be no a priori positivist explanation of human conduct in politics. "Conduct (and misconduct) is exclusively a human activity that is judged by a moral or legal standard of some kind."[34] This notion of practice has different origins. Next to Michael Oakshott's take on practice, MacIntyre's concept of virtues in his narrative political theory provide an ample characterization of a telic, which is a purposive, practice. MacIntyre defines practice as

> any coherent and complex form of socially established cooperative human activity through which goods internal to that form of activity are realized in the course of trying to achieve those standards of excellence which are appropriate to, and partially definitive of, that form of activity, with the result that human powers to achieve excellence, and human conceptions of the ends and goods involved, are systematically extended.[35]

The method, required by such a framework, then is to get the hands dirty by digging into archives; looking at foreign office documents, memoirs, and newsprints; and conducting interviews to grasp the notion of practice, self-conception, and the discourses of self-justification of the actors involved.[36] In other words, classical Realism is an intersubjective and sociological approach to study politics that strives beyond the mainstream assumption of the primacy of structure over agency (particularly attributed to the English School today).[37] Classical Realism does not simply rely on the Hobbesian tradition of power as a means of self-preservation.[38] Rather for Morgenthau, power is a "psychogenic condition which rested on inter-subjective relations . . . power was for Morgenthau generally created through the interaction of people: as a result and quality of human action."[39]

Morgenthau's notion of power is comparable to Hannah Arendt's. Arendt defined power as a product of action arising between people. Therefore, only a group can possess power. Once the group breaks down, so does power. Arendt is thus critical of the Aristotelian notion of the inherently political human being (i.e., the *zoon politicon*) as one person alone can never be political.[40] Based on similar assumptions, Morgenthau stressed the importance of observing humans' position among their fellows. In his fragments of an autobiography, Morgenthau distanced himself from the Freudian influence (which he attributed as "reductionism") that apparently resonates the term "desire."[41] Still, the desire for power is a constant element in Morgenthau's work. This is obvious in *Politics among Nations*, which translates the desire for power into international political conduct via the three political forms of the politics of the status quo, the politics of imperialism, and the politics of prestige.[42] In social life, in other words, "the principle of desire is translated into the lust for power," reflected in the three aforementioned expressions.[43]

Particularly in the case of Morgenthau's Realism, epistemological assumptions easily become complicated, leading to accusations of Realism as a positivist enterprise. This is a rather obvious accusation as Morgenthau himself declared certain objective laws of international politics. Such a view, however, conflates Morgenthau's ontological view and methodological choice. For Morgenthau those laws are what ideal types are for Max Weber.[44] They are concepts to idealize reality and do not correspond to, let alone display, reality. Ideal types, maxims, or reflections are instruments of understanding, to give meaning to the objects under study. Realism thus does not assume an epistemological separation between the subject (i.e., International Relations) and its objects (i.e., international politics).[45] Clifford Geertz summarized for his anthropological approach of culture what holds true for Morgenthau as well, including important proceedings for the methodological approach of this book:

> Believing, with Max Weber, that man is an animal suspended in webs
> of significance he himself has spun, I take culture to be those webs, and
> the analysis of it to be therefore not an experimental science in search of
> law but an interpretive one in search of meaning. . . . Operationalism as a

methodological dogma never made much sense so far as the social sciences are concerned, and except for a few rather too well-swept corners—Skinnerian behaviorism, intelligence testing, and so on—it is largely dead now. But it had, for all that, an important point to make, which, however we may feel about trying to define charisma or alienation in terms of operations, retains a certain force: if you want to understand what a science is, you should look in the first instance not at its theories or its findings, and certainly not at what its apologists say about it; you should look at what the practitioners of it do.[46]

Conclusion

Abductive research logic illustrates the comprehensiveness of this amalgam of qualitative research methods and an interpretative epistemology. Abduction's typical situation is

> when we become interested in a class of phenomena for which we lack applicable theories. We simply trust, although we do not know for certain, that what we see is not random. We collect pertinent observations while applying concepts from existing fields of our knowledge. Instead of trying to impose an abstract theoretical template (deduction) or "simply" inferring propositions from facts (induction), we start reasoning at an intermediate level (abduction).[47]

Abduction highlights a nonlinear research logic (instead of a "first this, then that" logic), constantly going "back and forth in an iterative-recursive fashion between what is puzzling and possible explanations for it."[48] The focus on agential political conduct as presented here certainly struggles with what is asked for today in academia and the policy-making world: problem-solving approaches that reduce theory to a problem-solving social endeavor. The epistemological pitfalls of the latter route are particularly vexing in current International Relations literature that sets out to solve puzzles.[49] For Realism, what International Relations needs are theoretical approaches of how to frame, understand, and explain beyond merely explaining by naming actors and their practices.[50] Classical Realists, then, are also problem solvers because they oppose a rationalist framework, yet at the same time helping to solve *how to think about* international politics. Doing so along a nonlinear research logic is particularly tempting if we have a closer look at two main streams of thought: Realism and mimetic theory.

2.

Desire for Power
and the Power of Desire

nderstanding International Relations as a form of practical philosophy, rather than an offspring of social science, means, foremost, an understanding of the entanglement between political theory and political practice.[1] It is not least therefore that such an approach of theorizing political phenomena in the international realm coincidences with core assumptions of mimetic theory. Taking the assumptions of mimetic theory regarding the international serious warrants the use of this theory in international political analysis and, at the same time, illustrates why mimetic theory is a helpful tool rather than a meta-theory. A first assumption, as mimetic theory reminds International Relations, is that international society is not based on some kind of a social contract. That societies work or function on the basis of some kind of social contract—that people literally sat down and talked out the rules, which is an act of reason or will—remains a persistent illusion mainly because it explains how societies work but not why they are what they are.[2] Skepticism of the autonomous individual is a second major assumption of mimetic theory with grave consequence for theorizing international politics. This is perhaps Girard's own most paramount verdict and of grave consequences for social sciences and practical philosophy alike. Unfortunately, it is rarely outspoken and far from self-evident in terms of description in his work.[3]

I argue that the insights of mimetic theory enrich thinking about Self, Other, and identity in International Relations theory within the theoretical framework of Realism and particularly within the work of Hans Morgenthau. Bringing Girard's and Morgenthau's thoughts into discussion illustrates that Morgenthau's thoughts point toward insights delivered by Girard's mimetic theory as well.[4] Most often, however, these theoretical underpinnings of Realism remain outspoken and implicit. What is more, turning to mimetic theory sheds light on what Morgenthau addressed in the "laws that govern human nature" but seldom made explicit: the importance of desire and imitation in human conduct.[5]

Despite the similarities between mimetic theory and Morgenthau's Realism, there are only few attempts to make use of Girard's mimetic theory for International Relations.[6] Mimetic theory is a diverse and contested field in the social sciences and humanities, and Girard's version is certainly contested.[7] Part of the reason for the disinterest of many social science subjects is that Girard's version of mimetic theory is essentially a Christian anthropology. It consists of three core elements: mimetic desire, the scapegoat mechanism as the origin of culture, and a theory of religion emphasizing the difference between pagan myth and the Biblical revelation.[8] The former archbishop of Canterbury, Rowan Williams, captures the essence of Girard's mimetic theory as

> something like a "novelistic" version of human origins—a bid for a narrative that will allow all of us to "read" our human experience differently and with greater honesty or truthfulness. And it is important to say—in the light of some critical comments in recent discussion—that, like a novel (indeed, arguably like Jewish-Christian scripture as well), this does not of itself endorse, let alone sacralize, what it narrates: it seeks to induce a kind of recognition that makes possible a different narrative. Girard provides not only a narrative of origins but also a narrative—the Christian narrative of a radically nonviolent deity—that equips us to recognize what we would rather not recognize because it simultaneously opens a new path.[9]

In the following, I rely on the first two elements pointed out by Williams. Already Plato and Augustine stressed the interdependence between imitation and desire: we always imitate what we admire.[10] Religious traditions and doctrines not only understand the connection between imitation and religion. They are also aware of the dangers that come along with imitation if it turns into envy. In the Biblical tradition, it is the tenth commandment of the Decalogue that shows this awareness most clearly. Girard strongly emphasized the importance of this Biblical text. "The Christian tradition has also always emphasized the longing for God as our highest good—our *summum bonum*—as a way to overcome and avoid envious rivalry."[11] For Girard, mimetic rivalry is the main cause of interpersonal violence. He denies the Rousseauean belief of the natural amicability of humans as well as theories that assume a natural (instinctive) aggressive human drive.[12]

Girard uses the Greek term *mimesis* to point to the connection between desire and imitation. However, it is not the desire for a definite or original object but to follow the desire of others.[13] *Imitation* therefore does not simply mean to copy others. What is desired is socially constructed and occurs in a "triangular desire," consisting of the Self, the Other ("mediator"), and the object that is desired by the subject.[14] This is "because the person knows, imagines, or suspects that the model or mediator desires it as well. Therefore, the goods or objects people desire, and their ideas about what to desire, are based on the ideas and desires they learn from others."[15] As long as the desired object is nonexclusive, such as education, mimetic rivalry may even lead to social improvement. Once an exclusive object is desired, mimetic rivalry potentially leads to violence.

Mimetic rivalry is particularly obvious in civil wars. The smaller the difference between people, the more they are fixated on it. Sigmund Freud called this the "Narcissism of minor differences."[16] Pierre Bourdieu as well outlined this conflictual trait of identity: "Social identity lies in difference, and difference is asserted against what is closest, which represent the greatest threat."[17] The genocide in Rwanda might serve as an illustration of this mechanism that mimetic theory points out. Tutsis were, due to many reasons (e.g., bonding with the colonial masters and distribution of resources), in better social, political, and economic positions than the Hutus. Hence, "these satisfiers became Objects of mimetic desire on the part of Hutus. It is easy to see that this desire for the Objects was an ontological desire to be like the Tutsis—to be Tutsi."[18] People destroy what they most love and that civil war is indeed the "primary form" of war. The longing for recognition just where there is minor space for recognition is a prevailing feature, particularly in civil wars.[19] Hunger and despair, in fact, do not blur all the differences and do not make us all the same. Rather, as Victor Frankl observed, people became more differentiated.[20]

The bottom line of mimetic theory is that humans are not free to choose their desires or that desire is autonomous.[21] It is not because we find something charming and desirable but because others do so. Consequentially, desire has little to do with need. What humans need (i.e., to survive) is often different from their desires (e.g., recognition) that are prone for conflict.[22] If politics, as commonly assumed, would only be about the negotiation of the shortage of goods and institutions and individual choice, there would be no need for political science, and politics would be much more peaceful. A large portion of what makes mimetic theory alluring for political science and International Relations is the explanation it offers on violence. This explanation, however, refers neither to philosophical nor to biological insights but rather argues for a third social way of understanding human conduct—imitation.[23]

Since humans, unlike animals, are not restrained in violence (i.e., in following an instinct), unleashed mimetic desire may lead indeed to Hobbes's "war all against all." No instinctive brakes can prevent humans from destroying themselves. People do not fight because of differences, but because they are similar and they long for the same.[24] Mimetic desire, then, causes "disunity among those who cannot possess their common object *together*." In turn, mimetic desire creates "solidarity among those who can fight the same enemy *together*."[25] The blow of one of the rivals eventually fascinates others leading them to imitate this action in striking a weaker one. "The war of all against all suddenly becomes a war of all against one. The single victim is expelled or killed. Girard calls this unconscious, collective deed the *scapegoat mechanism*."[26] The world today, according to Girard, is in a state of a constant competition due to mimetic rivalry on a global scale. The consequence is a manifest danger of the escalation to extremes.[27] More often than not, the result of this spiral toward extremes is that humans no longer curse and then bless scapegoats. Rather, scapegoats today only get cursed.

Religion, Politics, and Mimetic Theory

One of the main purposes of culture as a custodian of order, following Girard's arguments, is the containment of mimetic rivalry. Girard's theory assumes the scapegoat mechanism as the origin of culture, meaning the spontaneous psychological mechanism when we accuse someone to be guilty of something. In a lengthy analysis of ancient literature and literary "figures of desire," Girard identifies the scapegoat as the origin of culture, since the scapegoat—the victim—is demonized and divinized at the same time.[28] The metaphysical foundation of religion, the sacred, which is blessed and cursed at the same time, is essential for the functioning of society.[29] This is because the scapegoat mechanism is a sacrificial substitution to protect society from its own inherent destructive tendencies due to mimetic rivalry.[30]

As one of the first social scientists, Scott Appleby pointed out this "ambivalence of the sacred" and its importance regarding international politics.[31] However, pointing to the ambivalence of religion is not sufficient for a social science analysis. First, religion certainly can be a source for conflict and for conflict transformation. It certainly can also "function" as neither of those two. Second, it is problematic, as some of the contemporary studies in religion and international relations do, to see religion, or even special branches of religion such as Christianity or Islam, as unified social phenomena. Although one tradition may share a certain, at least thin common theological standard, this does not mean that this is accepted or interpreted everywhere in the same way.[32]

Beyond its anthropological insights, mimetic theory's assumptions also call for a deeper religious discourse in the public as Jürgen Habermas called for. Scholars successfully applied this discourse to illustrate the diffusion of religious norms into a secular context and language via institutional translation.[33] However, secular language eliminates the originally religious aspect and produces irritations. When sin transforms into guilt, when misdoings against religious rules transforms into offense against secular-human law, something gets lost.[34] Girard himself attempts to limit "politics to make way of faith."[35] This is particularly evident in Girard's last major work in which he sets out to challenge, at the example of Raymond Aron, the assumed shortcomings of International Relations scientific (i.e., rationalistic) premises.[36]

Mark Juergensmeyer argues that religious nationalism holds the potential to start a new Cold War between religious groups and the secular West.[37] If this is true, then Girard's anthropological theory of violence can be of methodological use, since many theories of violence in the context of international politics rely on Max Weber's dictum of the state's legitimate use and monopoly of violence.[38] The state, Morgenthau wrote in 1945, "has become indeed a 'mortal God'" that "actually delimits the manifestations of the individual desire for power."[39] In international politics today, it seems that there are a growing number of battles between the sacred and the profane. This description traces back to Émile Durkheim's distinction between "the sacred and the profane," in other words, the sacred and the secular.[40] As a matter of time, Morgenthau was more worried of rising nationalism:

> For the claim to universality which inspires the moral code of one particular group is incompatible with the identical claim of another group; the world has room for only one, and the other must yield or be destroyed. Thus, carrying their idols before them, the nationalistic masses of our time meet in the international arena, each group convinced that it executes the mandate of history, that it does for humanity what it seems to do for itself, and that it fulfills a sacred mission ordained by providence, however defined. Little do they know that they meet under an empty sky from which the gods have departed.[41]

There is a tradition and practice in every world religion that through the adjustment toward the holy, the "sacred, human life can ban evil. "Evil," in this sense, refers to the mimetic desire that Girard calls the source of violence.[42] According to the theological element of Girard's theory, people have to recognize the importance of the rules laid out in the Decalogue, particularly the first commandment, which "addresses God who as our highest good enables us to reach mimetically out for him without being at the same time forced into envious destruction."[43] "The sacred," in terms of Girard, is sensitive of the violence arising out of mimetic rivalry. For mimetic theory, particularly monotheistic religious traditions are aware of the prevailing existence of violence. They teach what to do and what not to do in order to avoid the flaming up of violence based on mimetic rivalry.[44] Taking the Decalogue seriously and sticking to religious rituals transforms the violent scapegoat mechanism into a ritual one. This acknowledgement is supposed to lead to a life that does not end up in the deadlock of mimetic rivalry.[45]

For mimetic theory, the persistent pattern of mimetic desire is the source of "evil." Evil is thus potentially inherent to any political and social act. Morgenthau distinguishes between ethics and politics and solving it in practice by choosing the lesser evil.[46] He warned that just because evil is inherent to any political action, the "idea of the ethical end justifying unethical means leads to the negation of absolute ethical judgements all together."[47] Mimetic theory points International Relations toward the need for a relational ontology of human desire and political order. This is even more so if we rely on the hypothesis that *politics* "is social action that helps men to solve the tension between their needs and social facts."[48] International politics, consequently, is "the attempt of certain groups of individuals to solve the tensions between the needs of their own people and the social facts of others and the world."[49] There is, in other words, no conceptualization of political agency outside its structure. This is where classical Realism and its relational conceptualization of the political comes in.[50]

Realism and Mimetic Theory

Defining Realism, scholars emphasize skepticism, relationally, power, and power politics. There are at least three principles and core assumptions of Realism. First, human beings cannot survive as individuals but rather in groups. Group centricity and tribalism are facts of social and political interaction with which International Relations theory has to come to terms. Second, politics is a struggle, but it also represents cooperation between self-interested groups under the conditions of uncertainty and fear.[51] Third, power is a given in social and political interaction, and is a necessary requirement in order for groups to achieve their goals. Morgenthau argued, "the social sciences cannot hope to master the social forces unless they know the laws which govern the social relations of men."[52] Sixty years after Morgenthau's statement, Alexander Wendt claimed the same: that social theory must begin with some theory of the human nature.[53] Yet still, conventional wisdom has it that Morgenthau and Realism resemble a Machiavellian-Hobbesian approach, that is, foremost rationalist and positivist.

Girard's mimetic theory is one possible key for a better and more comprehensive understanding of Realism. Morgenthau's theoretical outlines point to the gap between assumptions of humans as "political animals by nature" and assumptions of humans as "moral animals." Contemporary political Realism tends to ignore this gap.[54] In an attempt to identify the social constructivist element in Realism, Samuel Barking, for example, characterizes power politics as relative, relational, and social: power politics are meaningful only in relation to other actors; targets of power are themselves actors; and social groups (i.e., states) wield power.[55] What is more, this view of Realism posits that political action is inherently (self) contradictory.[56] Politics produces meaning yet, at the same time, falls short to address the complexity of human nature, its contradictions, and tragedies.[57] "He who acts,'" Morgenthau approvingly cites Goethe, "'is always unjust; nobody is just but the one who reflects.' The very act of acting destroys our moral integrity."[58]

Classical Realism, then, conflates Neorealism's inevitable strive for survival in the anarchical international system. Whereas for Neorealism tragedy is the missing of an alternative to escape the anarchical international condition (i.e., the struggle for survival), for Realism the tragic character of international politics resembles the tragic "character of political choice."[59] Yet choose we must, and a mimetic lens on Realism helps to point out that we are not as autonomous in our choices as commonly assumed.

The premises of classical Realism beg several epistemological questions. A pressing one is whether its assumptions about agency and power can hold up to the mainstream dogma of the individual's autonomy given the complexity of human nature, its tragic condition, and the resulting tragic condition of international politics. I propose that what drives agency is not autonomy (i.e., due to an assumed rationality) but desire. This is not only a question of epistemology but also one of ontology. Brent Steele, for one, points out that "states pursue social actions to serve self-identity needs, even when these actions compromise their physical existence."[60] Those identity needs are also based on the imitation of the desire of others. Morgenthau, along with Reinhold Niebuhr, in his acknowledgement of emotions and change in politics, pushed "us to consider the protean forms of emotional agency fuelling political contestation across local and global levels."[61] Realism, then, transcends the separation of the levels of analysis, demanded by Neorealists and Constructivists alike.[62] Mimetic theory provides a pattern of taking emotional agency seriously as outlined by classical Realists. International Relations research, on the other side, only marginally touched this aspect.[63]

There are at least two factors that justify discussing the insights of mimetic theory and twentieth-century Realism in parallel. First, we are witnessing a revival of the synthesis of International Relations theories and political theory (e.g., political theology took a grasp of international political issues).[64] The global resurgence of religion almost forced new strings of discussion in International Relations theory.[65] Prominent philosophers—sometimes not genuine philosophers of religion—like Charles Taylor and his *A Secular Age* or Jürgen Habermas's discussion with Cardinal Ratzinger (later Pope Benedict XVI) touched on issues of religion and international politics.[66] A second factor propelling a discussion between Girard and Morgenthau is the growing relatedness between International Relations theories and domestic political issues, particularly regarding conflict.[67] Failed states and humanitarian intervention led to changes in thinking about international politics, placing a strong emphasis on global politics, global governance, and, consequently, on the Other and strangers.[68] Neorealism is about the third image—the international level—largely leaving aside, in Kenneth Waltz's terms, the first and second image, meaning man and the state.[69] Although Morgenthau and Waltz never meant to strictly divide between the domestic and the international or systemic level, this is the prevailing textbook consensus.[70] Recent scholarship on Realism, dealing with material, "hard fact," issues of international politics, also addresses the importance of cultural factors and identity-related variables.[71]

The "struggle for power among nations" Morgenthau had in mind, and which became synonymous for the Realist family of thought, is also the struggle for the imitation and desire among nations.[72] Seen from the Realist perspective, seeking gains such as the global common good by assumedly universal notions of justice and freedom is not a practice in politics.[73] Relative gains thus matter to Realism and mimetic theory, which becomes obvious when looking at their insights on conflict and political conduct. Already Thomas Hobbes pointed to the fatal consequences of mimetic rivalry in politics: "If any two men desire the same thing which nevertheless they cannot both enjoy, they become enemies, and in the way to their End . . . endeavour to destroy, or subdue one another."[74]

An interesting question about mimetic desire concerns the reasons why some societies are more prone to violence then others. That is, why do some societies manage to contain the mimetic desire more than others? Scholars of war and international politics have pointed to the politics of identity, explaining conflicts after the Cold War as a problem of in-groups and out-groups.[75] In particular, ethnic and religious conflicts such as in civil wars consist of elements that seem to have less in common with traditional material interests. The interests at stake often are of social, cultural, or religious nature. This does not mean that they are irrational, but their particular condition makes them "nasty, brutish, and long."[76] Anthropological approaches such as mimetic theory contribute more ways of understanding a more globally interconnected world—which is, according to Barry Buzan, on its way "from international to world society."[77] International politics, after all, are a realm of human experience.[78] A discussion between Girard and Realism helps to expound on problems of cultural foundations of international order and disorder, both inevitable within the "realm of human experience."

Quite some time before Girard, Raymond Aron acknowledged the anthropological insight that the difficulty of peace is more a problem of the humanness than the animalistic nature of man. In a chapter on the "roots of war as an institution," Aron ends his thoughts, like Girard, by addressing the dangers of uncontrolled mimetic rivalry not stopped by instinct. Only humans are capable of preferring their own truth to humiliation and revolt. The hierarchy between master and servant will never be definite: "Tomorrow the masters will not need the servants any longer and then they have the power to exterminate them."[79] Aron excluded violence (i.e., war) in the thermonuclear age as a defensible possibility of international politics. In the 1950s, Morgenthau realized that a straightforward Realist approach of (limited) war in the nuclear age was absurd and rejected it.[80]

Surprisingly, Girard criticizes Aron as too rational.[81] Aron pronounced his understanding of rationality and Enlightenment as follows: "The rationalist is not unaware of the animal impulses in man, and the passions of man in society. The rationalist has long since abandoned the illusion that men, alone or in groups, are reasonable. He bets on the education of humanity, even if he is not sure he will win his wager."[82] Probably the best attempt to pinpoint the discussion between Girard and his accusation of the blind rationality of political science, as illustrated in the example of Aron and International Relations theory, is Morgenthau's *Scientific Man vs. Power Politics*. The Realist who is still said to think only in terms of harsh power politics and enlightened rationality pointed out the misunderstandings of the philosophy of rationalism turning into an "instrument of social salvation:"

> The philosophy of rationalism has misunderstood the nature of man, the nature of the social world, and the nature of reason itself. It does not see that man's nature has three dimensions: biological, rational, and spiritual. By neglecting the biological impulse and spiritual aspirations of man it misconstrues the function reason fulfils within the whole of human existence, it distorts the problem of ethics, especially in the political field; and it prevents the natural sciences into an instrument of social salvation for which neither their own name nor the nature of the social world fits them.[83]

Girard might have put forward a theoretical framework of anthropology that inherently aims to abolish the need of political science and International Relations. Nonetheless, International Relations does address the issues Girard pointed to without much sympathy for International Relations.[84] For example, Morgenthau argued for the "autonomy of the political sphere" just as he argued for the autonomy of each other scientific subject. However, the defense of the autonomy of the political seems to imply that a Realist understanding of politics forbids applying morality or irrationality to politics in order to understand or shape them. In fact, when Morgenthau was thinking about power, particularly in the context of the national interest, he was always thinking about morality as well: humans are both animal longing for power and creatures with a moral purpose.[85] Morgenthau, moreover, pointed out that the state—an institutionalized form of a self-interested group—is essential but by no means self-sufficient. Therefore, this particular form of political interaction is open for change. Put differently, a striking attribute of Realism is its engagement with power. Although a rather elusive concept, Realism urges for the centrality of power in all aspects of life, as Morgenthau frequently stressed.[86] Changing trends in culture, on the other side, can influence the conduct of international politics and therefore power, as Girard emphasizes.

International Relations theory has come to terms with an already extensive body of literature dealing with the formation of the Self—according to Waltz, the first image—which is certainly intertwined with the other images.[87] However, Realists' third image—or structural—approaches to international politics also illustrate the danger of what Girard calls a constant competition due to mimetic rivalry on a global scale.[88] Robert Gilpin, for example, pointed out that international politics are not only about power but also about wealth.[89] Neoclassical Realists illustrate this point with regard to the globalization of economic growth, producing political confidence and national pride leading, eventually, to a conflicted "rise of the rest."[90] Desiring what others desire—such as economic growth and wealth—could be a point at which Girard's theoretical approach of mimetic desire and rivalry can meet the aspirations of "the rest." Increasing globalization and the continuing intertwining of the three images, the vanishing of differences, not the "clash" of them may lead to greater potential for future conflict.[91] In terms of mimetic theory, not difference but sameness is the problem. Rivalry emerges from "relative" rather than absolute "disadvantage."[92] Social, political and economic inequalities do not lead to conflict and violence, per se. Rather, the danger lies within the possibility that groups can compare themselves to their peers. Often, Girard pointed out the danger of comparison.[93] At this point, his mimetic theory meets the one of Carl Schmitt who had a strong impact on twentieth-century Realism, particularly on Morgenthau.

Mimetic rivalry becomes most intense if conflicts turn into conflicts over identity. The less difference between identity there is, the more accented any borderline must be. Often, conflicts over identify resemble the "Narcissism of minor differences."[94] Because we know best the ones that are closest to us, we likely compare ourselves with them, which opens potential space for conflict. Schmitt was aware of this facet of human conduct.[95] In his memoirs, he details his conception of "the enemy." He asks, "Who can I acknowledge as my enemy? Certainly only the one who can question myself. And only I, myself, or my brother can question me really. Every Other proves to be my brother and the brother proves to be my enemy. The enemy is our own question as *Gestalt*."[96] Similarly, Girard points to a different understanding of violence as assumed by the theory of in-groups and out-groups or the clash of civilizations.[97] The problem of violence is one within, not genuinely between, groups.[98] Morgenthau developed a different concept of the political to Carl Schmitt, instead relying on a model of intensity:[99] For Morgenthau, "*the political in the specific sense consists on the particular degree of intensity of the connection created by the state's will to power between its objects and the state.*[100] Politics is thus "never an either/or state of affairs, but always a matter of degree, necessarily depending on *how* intense—and *potentially* violent—a conflict had become."[101] He contends that *what* turns a matter into a political one is a contest for the will to power, either by maintaining it, increasing it, or demonstrating it.[102] In an attempt of explaining *why* this is the case, he pointed out the human trait of comparison.[103] Conflict "was a pervasive facet of human existence. Interstate conflict remained exceptional chiefly because it typically constituted a particularly intense—and thus explosive—form of antagonism. It was there that we most commonly encounter what Schmitt described as potentially violent conflicts between friend and foe."[104]

Two examples may illustrate this point: In the first example, Morgenthau, having a rather pessimistic view of the human nature, stated in the disarmament debate that people "do not fight because they have arms. They have arms because they deem it necessary to fight."[105] A second example is Morgenthau's sense of violence within and between societies. Modern societies (i.e., in states) condemn violence as a norm in the physical sense while struggling for power within the society. Nevertheless, all societies endure the killing of enemies in the struggle for power, for example, during war. Girard, Schmitt, and Morgenthau in due course address a simple but important observation regarding international politics: the relations *between* groups— either states or societies—are different from the relations *within* groups.[106] To understand this intense relationship within groups, the desire to prove oneself is a key, which leads us directly to a deeper engagement with Girard and the first "image," to human conduct.

The Desire to Prove Oneself

Both, Morgenthau and Schmitt relied on an interpretation of Hobbes's insights, built on the notion that if any two individuals desire the same thing, conflict is inevitable. Schmitt's and Morgenthau's theories are therefore aware of the problems of mimetic desire. This is especially obvious since both acknowledge the intensity of internal conflict, which is particularly the case in contemporary societies fostering the democratic dogma of egalitarianism.[107] Alexis de Tocqueville pointed out the dangers of Western Egalitarianism in his observations on the American democratic culture. "Whatever the general effort undertaken by a society to make its citizens equal, particular individual pride will always fuel attempts to escape this sort of levelling and efforts to generate somewhere some inequality that it might benefit by."[108] Thus, Tocqueville writes,

> As social conditions become more equal, the number of persons increases who, although they are neither rich nor powerful enough to exercise any great influence over their fellows. Have nevertheless acquired or retained sufficient education and fortune to satisfy their own wants. They own nothing to any man, they expect nothing from any man; they acquire the habit of always considering themselves as standing alone, and they are apt to imagine that their whole destiny is in their own hands. Thus, not only does democracy make every man forget his ancestors, but it hides his descendants and separates his contemporaries from him; it throws him back forever upon himself alone, and threatens in the end to confine him entirely within the solitude of his own heart.[109]

Throughout his career, Morgenthau remained a rather skeptic conservative. A turn to the status quo was most desirable for him.[110] His later leaning toward Aristotle illustrates this point even more.[111] Not "everyone is equal in their ability to rule."[112] Skepticism toward unquestioned societal equality always has been a conservative characteristic. Most importantly, it was necessary to prevent what unleashed desire can destroy, as pointed out earlier in the relative disadvantages in second image competitions. In 1945, three years before his seminal study *Politics among Nations* first appeared, Morgenthau wrote about the *animus dominandi*. In his piece "The Evil of Politics and the Ethics of Evil," his later famous term "lust for power" comes close to Girard's reflection on desire. Interestingly enough, Morgenthau described this "lust for power" as "desire for power" *in relation to others*:

> The other root of conflict and concomitant evil stems from the animus dominandi, the desire for power. This lust for power manifests itself as the desire to maintain the range of one's own person with regard to others, to increase it, or to demonstrate it. In whatever disguises it may appear, its ultimate essence and aim is in one of these particular references of one

person to others. Centered as it is upon the person of the actor in relation to others, the desire for power is closely related to the selfishness of which we have spoken but is not identical with it.[113]

Parallel to Girard's conception of mimetic rivalry, which illustrates the initiating point of mimetic desire beyond the concern of plain survival, a simple selfishness effort, the early work of Morgenthau points toward the same direction. Trusting Sigmund Freud, he identified two fundamental drives of human nature: the drive for self-preservation (*Selbsterhaltungstrieb*) and the drive to prove oneself (*Bewährungstrieb*).[114] As Morgenthau wrote, the desire for power

> concerns itself . . . with his position among his fellows once his survival has been secured. Consequently, the selfishness of man has limits; his will to power has none. For while man's vital needs are capable of satisfaction, his lust for power would be satisfied only if the last man became an object of his domination, there being nobody above or beside him, that is, if he became like God.[115]

Even more so, in *Science: Servant or Master*, Morgenthau contended, "all seek to assert themselves as individuals against the world by mastering it. It is only when they choose as their object other men that they enter the political sphere."[116] In the essay "Love and Power," Morgenthau elaborates that the "will of the object of his power mirrors his own."[117] Already in his unpublished essay "The Significance of Being Alone," Morgenthau paved the way toward his mutual understanding and interconnectedness of love and power in relation to desire:

> Power and love are intimately connected, the desire for one growing out of the fulfilled or frustrated desire for the other, one state shading imperceptibly into the other; and the longing for immortality. For the perpetuation of one's existence beyond its natural limits, intermingles with the desire for power and love.[118]

Realism, then, does not stand still at the mainstream interpretation of the Hobbesian tradition of power as a means for self-preservation. It acknowledges Girard's position that violence is not a genuine problem between groups but one within social groups. The simple selfishness instinct or will for survival has its limits. The desire for power, concerned with human's positions among their fellow human beings, has no limits and is therefore prone to escalation.

Girard sees the only escape from the violent potential of mimetic desire in a turn toward the recommendations of the Sermon on the Mount. Girard argues that the Biblical revelation, other than pagan myths, is directed toward unveiling the scapegoat mechanism in criticizing the collective prosecution of innocent scapegoats. In the flow of unveiled violence, it only produces a greater contagion of violence.[119] Turning to the Sermon on the Mount and the cultural mechanisms of Christianity as an escape from the scapegoat mechanism, resulting from mimetic desire, is not what Schmitt or Morgenthau would have accepted or recognized in the first place. In Schmitt's opinion, the demand to love one's enemy was a private one, having no connection whatsoever to the insuperable enmity between groups.[120] Morgenthau was convinced of the necessity of the distinction between the official and private sphere of politics in theoretical terms because Realism

> maintains that universal moral principles cannot be applied to the actions of states in their abstract universal formulation, but that they must be filtered through the concrete circumstances of time and place. The individual may say for himself: "*Fiat justitia, pereat mundus* (Let justice be done, even if the world perish)," but the state has no right to say so in the name of those who are in its care.[121]

Morgenthau's Realism, after all, is not a positivist explanation of international affairs. Rather, it stresses human and moral choices, even if they are tragic.[122] In doing so, Realism attempts to explore the tension between political and ethical imperatives.[123] In due course it is not surprising, although often overlooked, that Morgenthau, regarding religious norms, noted similar to Girard that

> the Decalogue is a code of ethical norms which cannot be derived from premises of rational utility. The concept of virtue as the sum of human qualities required by ethics bears no resemblance to the standard of

utilitarian rationality. . . . the ethical norms which men feel actually bound
to follow . . . endeavour to satisfy nonutilitarian aspirations.[124]

In a different manner, another prominent Realist, E. H. Carr, echoed
this observation. Relying on Fyodor Dostoevsky's thoughts, he stated, "'eter-
nal harmony' was too high if it included the sufferings of the innocent."[125]
Quite differently, current self-described Realists such as Robert Kaplan, a
promoter of the power politics aspect of Realism, go as far as requesting a
pagan ethos for leadership. Kaplan does not acknowledge the dangers of
unveiled violence as pointed out by mimetic theory.[126] Others, however, have
emphasized that in-group cohesion does not necessarily require out-group
hostility (i.e., produced by the scapegoat mechanism), that identities are far
more flexible than assumed, and that collective identities are overlapping
and not a coherent system.[127] In addition, the English School addresses these
problems. Based on its take of practice and human conduct, the English
School acknowledges the insights of the dangers in a standstill at the recognition of politics, especially international politics, as a friend-foe distinction.
In turning to cosmopolitanism, solidarists, for example, emphasize the individual over the interest of the state and pursue a solidarist society, as opposed
to a plural one.[128]

While looking to anthropological theories like mimetic theory, International Relations perhaps must bet, in the words of Aron, "on the education
of humanity, even if he is not sure he will win his wager."[129] The open-ended
discussion between mimetic theory and Realism can help International
Relations to pursue a better understanding of international politics and its
basic theoretical claims. That remains true even if an appreciation of Girard's
thoughts can only help to make implicit claims and theoretical assumptions of Realism—like Morgenthau's stressing of desire and the evolution of
power—more explicit.

Conclusion

In this chapter, I initiated a dialogue between Girard's mimetic theory and
Morgenthau's Realism. Realism addresses issues like the power of desire, just
as mimetic theory does. I illustrated that there are approaches in Girard's

work where a fruitful discussion with International Relations can set in. To that end, I pointed out similarities in the theoretical approaches of Girard's theory and the Realist tradition of International Relations. Knowing the wider framework of various approaches of International Relations theory, other than their genuine disciplinary sources, can help deepen our understanding and use of them. Girard offers insights that can help International Relations to pursue a better understanding of problems and basic assumptions of twentieth-century Realism, particularly about power and the political in the context of the three images.

An obvious example illustrating the power of desire is Realism's foreign policy advice, particularly in terms of great power politics. Realists calling for offshore balancing illustrate the need to act as a role model for others, leading by example and not by coercion. Sure enough, all great powers claim their spheres of influence; however, these spheres of influence are influential by way of effective management. In the end, soft power might be the more sustainable way to lead by example at the national or international level. Soft power, to get others unconsciously what you want them to do, is arguably a willful manipulation of mimetic desire.

I readily acknowledge the problematic equalization of human desire and the desire of political actors such as states. Such equalizations drift into a perception of methodological individualism.[130] What is desired (e.g., the pursuit of the national interest) is a result of imitating others. In the "human conduct in a world of states," it is unlikely that one state would or even could exclude itself from the framework of conducting politics in the mainstream way.[131] Therefore, it may be that, as Alexander Wendt argued, in an arena of contestation, the common denominator is to say that states are actors or persons, attributing those properties and qualities such as rationality, identities, interests, beliefs.[132] However, what constructivist attempts miss, is the recognition of the political nature of humans, which is, as I suggested here, a struggle for power caused by the desire for power.[133]

3.

A Realist Mimetic View on Reconciliation

"If reconciliation is to be reconciled with liberalism, it will only be when liberalism is at its most liberal," notes Daniel Philpott.[1] A mainstream Western, enlightened understanding of science, particularly social science, thus has to be exceedingly liberal (i.e., generous) to accept reconciliation as a *political* concept, worth being applied in post conflict theaters.[2] Most often, this is done in order to regain social cohesion of a community or to establish social cohesion in the first place. Indeed, reconciliation, a genuinely *theological* concept with a hardwired transcendental aspect built in, has come a long way from its traditional roots in religious practices to be acknowledged as a desirable political practice. The call for retributive justice (i.e., not punishment) is a pressing argument of liberals to oppose reconciliation as a substitute for conflict settlement, addressing structural conflict causes.[3]

Samuel Huntington's study of the third wave of democratization in the late twentieth century illustrates the applicability and use of reconciliation particularly in emerging democracies.[4] Reconciliation managed to work its way around the globe. The South African Truth and Reconciliation Commission (TRC) is only the most prominent example up to now. The TRC has spread around the world as a kind of role model or best practice model, also stressing the progressive aspect of national reconciliation in emerging democracies.[5] Despite the contestation over its political relevance, the concept of reconciliation has found its way into social science analysis because of its impact on political practice. In times of focusing on individual accountability and responsibility, it provides a means helping justice prevail on more societal levels than only on political leadership and international criminal justice.[6]

Those trends and applications notwithstanding, a naive look and understanding of reconciliation as a means to post-conflict settlement (aka a reconciliation between victim and perpetrator is good for political stability and helps to prevent future atrocities of the same kind) is misleading. This is because the prevailing liberal understanding of politics and political practice has several shortcomings, as discussed earlier.[7] Realism, according to Morgenthau, fundamentally holds that politics is a relational intercourse. Additionally, mimetic theory, according to Girard, illustrates that reconciliation in the context of political conflicts should address the conflictual—that is, mimetic attitudes prior to human intentions and assumed rational actors.[8] Bringing in Realism and mimetic theory to the discourse of reconciliation in conflicts causes anyone interested in reconciliation to think beyond the achievement of a simple reconciliation between victim and perpetrator. Reconciliation requires digging deeper into the fundaments of politics and human intercourse. Girard's mimetic theory and its engagement with today's frequent use of victimization around everyday political life, particularly conflict, sheds light on the dangers of moralization in politics—not least because it singles out individuals. Mimetic theory illustrates that conflictual mimesis occurs prior to the actual conflict, a fact that is likely forgotten in reconciliation's practice.

Reconciliation

Ever since the introduction of reconciliation as a means of governmental politics in the twentieth century (e.g., via the TRC), there remains a persistent prejudice against the practice of reconciliation in the secular political sphere. This is mainly because, at its core, reconciliation is a religious concept, even a sacrament in Catholic terms.[9] I follow Philpott's definition in the political context: "Reconciliation is a concept of justice, that is to say, a set of propositions that tell us who ought to do what to whom, for whom, and on behalf of whom and the reasons why. The central meaning of reconciliation is the restoration of right relationship."[10] It is the last part of this definition that makes further exploration into the very conception of reconciliation worthwhile: "the restoration of right relationship." Although often framed as a process that in practice it has to be as well, reconciliation is an end, not a means. It is the end of forgiveness, itself not contrary to justice but reflective of it.[11] The ultimate goal of forgiveness is reconciliation since forgiveness includes the "elimination of one's negative feelings toward the wrongdoer."[12] Nevertheless, while reconciliation's tendency to harmonize is an important and helpful instrument for diplomacy, it is actually an antagonism to politics. This is because of its inherent tendency toward conflict on its own. There are several central elements within a political order that need to be matched if reconciliation is to be successful (i.e., at the end of forgiveness). Those elements therefore "open up a space for politics between former enemies"; truth telling, accountability, reparation, repentance and forgiveness.[13]

Truth telling should take place within public bodies such as illustrated at the TRCs work in South Africa.[14] People involved with these commissions saw the victim not just as a violated citizen but also as a sufferer. The difference to a trial, where the aim is to decide between guilt and innocence, is that ignorance of the truth is itself part of injustice. It is thus necessary to practice truth telling within a public body. Truth telling is one of the fundamental religious practices on the way to reconciliation, because it is believed that telling the truth can set humans free.[15] Accountability amounts to punishment and therefore to retributive justice. Without accountability, reconciliation would be cheap. A direct consequence of accountability is reparation. This may also include monetary reparation (e.g., health care for the victims) and could therefore be assessed as a form of punishment. Repentance means that the offender has openly (e.g., in front of a public body) expressed his or her sorrows to pave the way for forgiveness (e.g., President Bill Clinton's apology to Rwanda for failing to intervene during the genocide).[16] Forgiveness mirrors repentance, expressed explicitly if it is to be a constitutive element of reconciliation. Two things are important to note, one in terms of theory and one in terms of the political practice of reconciliation. First, all elements have the restorative purpose in common.

Second, so far only South Africa's TRCs applied all five dimensions of reconciliation in praxis.[17]

In moral terms, reconciliation refers to the restoration of a wrongdoer to a community.[18] In political terms, referring to Schmitt and his friend-enemy distinction of the political, to reconcile means to resolve or to settle.[19] That means that reconciliation is always limited by the very nature of the friend-enemy distinction (and therefore the conflictual nature of politics), implying the pluralism of political realities. Because plurality is placed in the source of a higher unity (i.e., God), it cannot be fully accorded to a political understanding and a traditional understanding of politics. The ideal is to heal and to harmonize. It seems to be impossible that reconciliation can match its ideals in a political world guided by a friend-enemy distinction. Therefore, it is necessary to develop an ethical concept of the political. Reconciliation can push that attempt forward through practice. Nevertheless, "political reconciliation must be conditioned by an awareness of its own impossibility."[20]

As outlined before, Carl Schmitt was everything but a liberal thinker. Nonetheless, liberalism has its own problems accepting reconciliation as a proper instrument in diplomatic or domestic affairs. There are four main points against it as a political instrument from a liberal perspective: liberals argue (1) for retributive justice, including some sort of punishment, (2) that reconciliation is a personal rather than a political affair, (3) that reconciliation is a religious concept and can therefore not be adapted to secular politics, and (4) reconciliation's divisiveness suggests that it could undermine social unity.[21]

However, the way from forgiveness to reconciliation to the reestablishment of harmony in a community in practice seems to trump liberal concerns. Reconciliation is not genuinely designed to eliminate guilt.[22] Regardless of whether it is a religious concept or technique, it also matches secular communal problems. Moreover, its aim is to promote rather than undermine social unity and harmony. It is important to note that successful reconciliation includes justice as a constitutive element. It would be wrong to assume a cheap reconciliation in which the part of forgiveness would argue as if the sins were not there.[23] Reconciliation, then, "should never be advanced through general amnesties" since forgiveness does not replace justice.[24] Rather, to "forgive outside justice is to make no moral demands; to forgive after justice is not to be vindictive.[25] In the case of the TRC, for example, by focusing on human-rights violations, which were by their very nature extreme (and, even in South Africa, illegal), the TRC neglected the more banal evils that sustained apartheid—the myriad ways in which everyday life itself was an insult to, indeed a negation of, human rights and human dignity. The hearings may, paradoxically, have thus enabled a majority of whites—who, after all, were not criminals or sadists themselves, merely beneficiaries of a criminal, sadistic system—to wall themselves off from responsibility.[26]

Reconciliation's Political Quality

Arendt was one of the first political thinkers in the twentieth century who came to appreciate the importance of reconciliation in the context of politics.[27] Arendt acknowledged the importance of reconciliation even if it is the ethical power of nonreconciliation and revenge, as in the case of Adolf Eichmann.[28] As pointed out earlier, reconciliation always operates at the "border between theological and political praxis."[29] It is thus, per definition, not a private enterprise. In order to qualify reconciliation within the context of the political, I first outline two approaches of a definition of the political. The first approach and arguably most prevalent one determines the political sphere by the separation of "us" and "them." Schmitt prominently outlines this approach of the political in his dualism between friend and enemy.[30] Schmitt's *Concept of the Political* is often misunderstood as a demonizing one. However, as Schmitt makes clear, what he calls the enemy is not necessary a bad or evil person. He is just the Other. This dualistic distinction certainly invites for speculation and misuse.

If politics is understood in Schmittian terms, any attempt of reconciliation is doomed to fail since the concept rests on an absolute distinction. Reconciliation thus can be seen as taking part in political responsibility. That also means that the practice of reconciliation in international politics runs counter to the trend of holding individuals accountable and responsible (e.g., for war crimes) despite structural influence or the fact that such gross crimes can never be pursued by individuals alone.[31] This is not least because some evil indeed may not be forgivable but reconcilable just because reconciliation deals with the individual and not his acts.[32]

Morgenthau developed a similar but nevertheless different approach of the political, deserting Schmitt's dualistic notion and instead relying on the degree of intensity.[33] The political has, according to Morgenthau, no fixed ground. Rather, it "depends on circumstances of time and place and does not result from a ground of principle."[34] Anything can become political. Realism thus opens a political gap to comprehend and value reconciliation—since any human relationship is potentially political. Morgenthau and other Realists relied on a genuine social understanding and theorizing of politics. Realism frees international politics from their static mainstream assumption—be it in terms of Schmitt's us versus them or liberal attempts of finding technocratic (i.e., rationalistic) solutions to political problems.[35] This is obvious in Morgenthau's concept of power and the consequent struggle for power, which essentially streams from the desire for power that concerns itself with comparing positions among others.[36] The Realist core assumption is not simply the "national interest defined in terms of power" for the purpose of self-preservation.[37] The essential human struggle for power concerns itself foremost with our own position among our followers. Politics, thus, operates at the borderline to the private sphere. Political action is inherently contradictory. On the one side, it is self-constituting and produces meaning; on the other side, it falls short of the complexity of human nature.[38] For Morgenthau's Realism, then, those who act are always unjust because "'nobody is just but the one who reflects.' The very act of acting destroys our moral integrity."[39]

Publicity in the political sphere, as it turned out in the experience around the TRC in Rwanda, is a necessary element for successful reconciliation.[40] Individual agency takes shape only in and due to sociality.[41] "The very notion of an individual moral agent presupposes the existence of a collective practice with its associated ethic embedded in it."[42] The political quality of reconciliation requires the public to be present and witness. The important distinction between political and personal realms applies similarly to the concept of reconciliation. Personal reconciliation, simply stated, involves a common understanding among individuals, a particular victim, or co-victim, and a particular offender. It is limited to the boundaries of the private sphere and is not inherently related to, nor does it affect, others on a broad public level. Considering reconciliation at the political level is more difficult to isolate. Most broadly, political reconciliation is a moral consensus, as it involves a common understanding and recognition of an event that took place between two conflicting sides.[43] Realism's conception of politics thus defies Schmitt's antagonistic conception.[44]

Liberal internationalism is one of Realism's major concerns and worries within the international realm. Because Realism builds its theory upon a social theory based on human interaction, this tradition is open to nonliberal concepts such as reconciliation.[45] That is not to say that there is a clear-cut distinction between Realism's conception of human "nature" and human "condition." Interpretations of Morgenthau's thought on this reach from the Jewish tradition over Aristotle to Sigmund Freud and many others. With this invoking of Realism, it becomes clear that this particular tradition of thinking of international politics and, moreover, its unit and individual level of analysis, is far more progressive regarding interpersonal political ambitions such as reconciliation as commonly assumed.[46]

Reconciliation and Mimetic Theory

Taking a closer look at violence on the global scale, various acts of violence reveal themselves as largely taking place within, rather than between, societies. One explanation for this distinctive feature of violence is that mimesis overreaches because people find it easier to compare themselves with their peers. Just like commercials make us believe that we all can achieve the same goals, status, and goods, the offspring of civil war are likely to follow the same mechanisms.

The largest genocide since the end of the Second World War in Rwanda dramatically illustrates this. Because of Tutsis often better social position (e.g., bonding with the colonial masters, resources) "these satisfiers became Objects of mimetic desire on the part of Hutus. It is easy to see that this desire for the Objects was an ontological desire to be like the Tutsis—to be Tutsi."[47] Empirical and theoretical research on revolutions supports this route of explanation based on mimetic theory.[48] It is not because people are poor that they revolt. Rather, they revolt after they experience an improvement in living conditions. The relative deprivation drives the "gap between what people feel rightfully entitled to and what they are capable of achieving under existing circumstances."[49] Mimetic theory buttresses these empirical findings. The more options there are to imitate, the more likely it becomes that people struggle to achieve and consequently rival over them. The "Narcissism of minor differences" turns out to cause conflict, not the large differences once there has been a relative improvement in the living condition.[50] The closer people are to each other, the harder it is to find a difference and the closer the threat grows. Realism and mimetic theory meet in their appreciation of reconciliation in the observation that "the moralization of politics has also driven the mimetic spiral of polarity."[51]

Liberal internationalism's moralization of politics has come a long way since its awakening after the First World War. Particularly the period after the Cold War has shown that worldwide intervention on liberal grounds became intermingled with humanitarian concerns.[52] The rising of a global justice movement by the end of the Cold War also propelled the quest for reconciliation as a means for a suitable post-conflict settlement.[53] Current trends of reconciliation efforts largely do away with their embedding in grand narratives—sometimes at great peril.[54] Realism believes in the political quality of global political interaction beyond political institutions, processes, and structures, in other words, in the primacy of politics in international politics.

Mimetic theory, on the other side, senses uneasiness because the enforcement of the liberal peace idea and the entrepreneurship of global justice and its democratic and egalitarian dogma lead to a mimetic crisis.[55] Often, the experience of a social and political improvement harbors more conflict.[56] The more freedom and equality humans are able to imitate, the more they expect. If left unfulfilled, these expectations potentially humiliate everyone.[57] This in turn fuels the potential for a mimetic crisis. On the other side, it is necessary to acknowledge that reconciliation is a far wider approach than the idea of liberal peace and a liberal stress on human rights.[58] Still, the prevailing notion that mimetic theory teaches us on the process as well as the events that eventually lead to reconciliation is that there are fewer differences between humans than we think there are. What is true for the mimetic crisis at the international level also holds true for the individual and domestic level:

> It is not surprising that in the era of globalization ... when wars are increasing, mimetism has gained ground since 1945 and is taking over the world. Everyone now knows that the looming conflict between the United States

and China, for example, has nothing to do with a "clash of civilizations," despite what some might try to tell us. We always try to see differences where in fact there are none.[59]

Despite the long-term trend that the world is becoming a less violent and instead a safer place, we are increasingly witnessing the spontaneous outbreak of uncontrolled violence.[60] This is true for the suburbs of Western cities, in the southern hemisphere and within the context of intra religious and intra ethic violence. Violence against one's fellow human being—civil and civic war—is indeed the "primary form of war" and is as prevailing as ever.[61] One trend that we can identify around the world where violence erupts is that it certainly owes a great deal to humiliation. Frantz Fanon, for one, described the Algerian anti-colonialist struggle primary as one waged due to humiliation and not due to hunger.[62] In *Talking to the Enemy*, Atran observes nothing less than this phenomenon—the experience of the witness of humiliation likely accelerates people's alternation to extremism.[63] There certainly is a growing need and demand for reconciliation after the outbreak of violent conflict and for the healing of past atrocities. Even more so, as the first major reconciliation projects in the twentieth century illustrate, reconciliation is often asked for during the transition of political systems. The greatest hindrance for any reconciliation process is the human desire for revenge.[64] Realism and mimetic theory are aware of this fact, so was Arendt. Her conclusion from witnessing Adolf Eichmann's trial was that he must die.[65]

Conclusion

In this chapter I illustrated the complexity of desire and the interdependent social relations affected by it. Reconciliation is likely to be successful when the antagonists become aware of their interdependence.[66] Yet it is an interdependence that must step aside from judicial approaches of reconciliation alone, for example relying on reciprocity.[67] Moreover, "Models of reconciliation based on legal distinctions or acknowledgment of rights underestimate how sacred causes and true beliefs deny the other's humanity."[68] It is thus not surprising that scholars have identified the great, although rarely used potential of the institutionalized religions (i.e., churches) in the process of reconciliation.

In *The Brothers Karamazov*, Fyodor Dostoevsky recalls the limits of reconciliation and its political quality. The answer to the question of what we can do against the evil perpetrated in the world is that we should protest against it in order to make sure that no harmonization attempts to make "evil into something to forget or something to serve some final triumph of good on earth, in heaven, or in hell."[69] Thus, in *The Brothers Karamazov*, the character of Ivan pledges:

> How are you going to atone for them? Is it possible? But what do I care for avenging them? What do I care for a hell for oppressors? What good can hell do, since those children have already been tortured? And what becomes of harmony, if there is hell? I want to forgive. I want to embrace. I don't want more suffering. And if the sufferings of children go to swell the sum of sufferings which was necessary to pay for truth, then I protest that the truth is not worth such a price. I don't want the mother to embrace the oppressor who threw her son to the dogs! She dare not forgive him! Let her forgive him for herself, if she will, let her forgive the torturer for the immeasurable suffering of her mother's heart. But the suffering of her tortured child she has no right to forgive, what becomes of harmony? Is there in the whole world a being who would have the right to forgive and could forgive? I don't want harmony. For the love of humanity I don't want it. I would rather be left with unavenged suffering. I would rather remain with my unavenged suffering and unsatisfied indignation, *even if I were wrong*. Besides, too high a price is asked for harmony; it's beyond our means to pay so much to enter on it. And so I hasten to give back my entrance ticket, and if I am an honest man I am bound to give it back as soon as possible. And that I am doing. It's not God that I don't accept, Alyosha, only I most respectfully return Him the ticket.[70]

Realism's view on reconciliation cautions, along the lines of the Aristotelian notion of virtues, that politics it is not about the last questions of how a perfect society would or should look like. It is, as least as importantly, about the day-to-day practice of living a good life—ethical compromises included. Mimetic theory, taken seriously in normative terms, first, shows that there are fewer differences among humans than we wish them to be. Second, mimetic theory leads to the conclusion—particularly when looking at "successful" reconciliation efforts (including healing processes and accomplished forgiveness)—that the consequence must be to strictly refuse violence in the first place, let alone harmonize or humanize it.[71]

4.

Dag Hammarskjöld—International Civil Service and Mimesis

The Swedish second secretary-general of the United Nations (1953–1961) Dag Hammarskjöld (1905–1961) is a modern example illustrating the positive effects that a religious ethical framework can have, opposing the widespread fear of actors motivated by religion. Hammarskjöld's uniqueness lies within his rationality, characterized by a realistic notion of politics and the conduct of his political agency as secretary-general of the United Nations (UN).[1] His mystical private life was not discovered until after his death, when his diary *Markings* was found and published posthumously.[2] Hammarskjöld referred to *Markings* as his "*white book* concerning my negotiations with myself—and with God" and wrote that it was "the only true 'profile' that can be drawn."[3] Although most times ignored or overlooked, it "is impossible to understand the statesman Hammarskjöld absent his moral convictions." Rather, "it is possible to generalize that Hammarskjöld's ethical framework also influenced both his international political agenda and his method of administration."[4] The life and legacy of Hammarskjöld possess some of the most important elements of international affairs such as questions of war and peace. He is also an example of the significance of individuals and leadership in international affairs.[5] In the case of the UN secretary-general, it was the "call to promote a global ethic [that] falls most squarely . . . on the shoulders

41

of the secretary-general as the head of the UN system."[6] This promoted global ethic, lying on the shoulders of the secretary-general, was founded in and influenced by a mystical experience that, he holds in *Markings* is

> always *here* and *now*—in that freedom which is one with distance, in that stillness which is born of silence. But—this is a freedom in the midst of action, a stillness in the midst of other human beings. The mystery is a constant reality to him who, in this world, is free from self-concern, a reality that grows peaceful and mature before the receptive attention of assent. In our era, the road to holiness necessarily passes through the world of action.[7]

Hammarskjöld is an example of how "diplomatic theory and practice can be informed and enriched by experimenting with spirituality," an often forgotten or ignored aspect of diplomacy.[8] I set out to answer Costas Constantinou's question of whether we are "willing to innovate with and politicise discourses that reflect on the spiritual dimension of Otherness and its value in knowing the Self?"[9] What guides the chapter in answering this question is the value of understanding diplomats belief systems in managing conflicts when "the juxtaposition of two mutually exclusive versions of truth is arguably the greatest enemy of diplomacy."[10] Hammarskjöld's legacy as a diplomat and an international civil servant in particular, it turns out, draws on the Realist tradition of international relations that, outlined by Morgenthau, "combines the importance of judgment, the need to act on the basis of those judgments, and a self-knowledge that can allow for morality and self-interest to sit side by side."[11] However, it is also mimetic theory and its insights into Realist premises that opens up a more comprehensive understanding of Hammarskjöld's legacy.

The Mystic and Diplomat Hammarskjöld: Realistic Optimism

An "ethical framework can be defined as the combination of personal values that establish the beliefs, forms of reasoning, and interpretations of the world that guide an individual when making judgments about proper behavior in specific contexts."[12] There is a nearly endless body of literature approaching definitions of mystics. Bernard McGinn, for example, defines "the mystical element in Christianity [as] that part of its belief and practices that concerns the preparation for, the consciousness of, and the reaction to what can be described as the immediate or direct presence of God."[13] More adequately, particularly regarding the person of Hammarskjöld, is the definition and distinction of Gnostic spirituality and erotic-mystics or *agape*, outlined by Fred Dallmayr:

> In essence, gnostic spirituality culminates in the recognition of one's own basic unity or identity with the godhead, hence in a form of deification. It is chiefly on this point that erotic-mystical or, *agape*, spirituality demurs. By not accepting the radical dualist scenario, erotic spirituality also refuses to endorse its telos or cosmic teleology. In lieu of the eventual conquest or erasure of the world by the divine, *agape* stresses the mediated and covenantal relation between the two shores; accordingly, the gnostic path of deification or self-deification is here replaced by the ascending path of loving redemption.[14]

Hammarskjöld's mysticism was influenced by the Jewish philosopher Martin Buber and the German protestant theologian and physician Albert Schweitzer, as well as by the Christian tradition of the *Imitatio Christi* by the mystics Tomas à Kempis, St. John of the Cross, and Meister Eckhart. The morality of Hammarskjöld "goes beyond the public-private distinction. It is best explained as a three-way exchange between one's own personal communication with God, God's influence on the mundane world (manifest in public service), and the personal divinity that one applies there as well."[15] Shortly before his death, Hammarskjöld had started translating Buber's *I and Thou*. He agreed with his mentor Buber "that a separation of politics and spirit was a sin against the spirit as well as a sin against politics."[16] Hammarskjöld's fondness for the philosopher Buber is not surprising. "In every case, Christian *agape* spirituality involves a loving relationship between an 'I' and a 'You' . . . between humans and the divine."[17] Hammarskjöld's own words capture his take on medieval mysticism best in the context of his understanding of serving as an international civil servant who "is active as an instrument, a catalyst, perhaps an inspirer—he serves."[18] But to fulfil this duty as someone who serves the international community, it is necessary to say yes to every demand and fate:

But the explanation of how man should live a life of active social service in full harmony with himself as a member of the community of the spirit, I found in the writings of those great medieval mystics for whom "self-surrender" had been the way to self-realization, and who in "singleness of mind" and "inwardness" had found strength to say *yes* to every demand which the needs of their neighbours made them face, and to say *yes* also to every fate life had in store for them when they followed the call of duty.[19]

One characteristic of Hammarskjöld's spirituality is that it is compatible with a reasonable ethical framework one would expect from a Western socialized diplomat. He was convinced that reason can be a starting point for mystics and that mystic can lead to reason.[20] "For Hammarskjöld, mystics are real flesh and blood persons who have chosen to risk a lifetime in service."[21] John of the Cross, who Hammarskjöld's intensively studied and meditated on, stressed the active and rational component of *agape*:

As John [of the Cross] himself elaborates: "Our soul becomes unified with God not through cognition of mental representations, nor through passive enjoyment or anything sensual, but intellectually only through faith, recollectively through hope, and actively through love"—where *love* means an ecstatic movement towards the "You" of God and also laterally toward the "You" of fellow human beings.[22]

For Hammarskjöld, mystics must not be detached from the real world or become an end in itself. On his search for universal principles, he draws from his personal mystic, with its basic concepts of love, patience, justice, and prudence, to concrete political activity. He was well aware of the classical mystical dictum, which can already be found in the John of the Cross's *Imitatio Christi*: "'If you rely on yourself alone, nothing is accomplished; but if you rely on God, heaven's grace redeems you.'"[23] This is also reflected in *Markings*:

"Treat others as ends, never as means." And myself as an end only in the capacity as a means: to shift the dividing line in my being between subject and object to a position where the subject, even if it is in me, is outside and

above me—so that my *whole* being may become an instrument for that
which is greater than I.[24]

Alynna Lyon summarizes Hammarskjöld's ethical framework as one formed
by the triangular construction of his spirituality with God, the spirituality
in his private life, and his spirituality regarding the perception of his public
service:

> The first involves his own spiritual relationship with God (coram Deo).
> Spirituality in his private life (coram hominibus) provides the second pil-
> lar. Spirituality in his public service (coram mundo) provides the third.
> Within this triad there are several layers, beginning with his personal con-
> victions and broadening out to the public sphere. Faith, receptivity, and
> acceptance are the core principles that set a foundation for all other engage-
> ments. His ethical framework, then, holds public service, self-sacrifice, and
> neutrality as more public manifestations of the first stratum. From here his
> personal convictions broaden out to include more community-oriented
> values. . . . The final dimension really takes shape through his service as
> secretary-general. The values of peaceful resolution of conflict, economic
> opportunity, political equality, and international justice are manifestations
> of his more personal operational code.[25]

There are several baselines of Hammarskjöld's professional ethical framework: to serve in awe of life, integrity, universality, solidarity, and optimism,
and the importance of comprehensive standards in culture, literature, and
politics. What is remarkable while having a closer look at the basics of Hammarskjöld's ethical framework is that, despite the often claimed pessimism
of mysticism, he remained optimistic. This aspect becomes especially significant in considering Hammarskjöld's accomplishments as secretary-general.

Hammarskjöld's efforts during his tenure as secretary-general illustrate
his realistic perception of the bigger picture as recommended by ethical Realism. Still, as a former (impartial) politician, he was also aware of the "tem-
poral perspective" in ethics.[26] Hammarskjöld's ethical framework influenced
his administrative duties (e.g., in his opposition to McCarthyism) as well as
his diplomatic efforts in several international crises (e.g., the U.S.-Chinese

dispute in 1954, the Suez Canal crisis, or the peacekeeping mission in the
Congo). He was neither a genuine idealist nor a realist. For him, mystical
belief was characterized by practical political engagement. Due to his neutral engagement in political crises during the Cold War, he was rejected by
governments in the East and in the West alike.[27] One of Hammarskjöld's
most prominent legacies is silent or private and preventive diplomacy as well
as the UN's military engagement (blue-helmet missions). Hammarskjöld
"regarded the United nations as a mission."[28] Lord Gladwyn, the first acting
secretary-general of the UN, describes Hammarskjöld's intellectual way of
dealing with problems as follows:

> The majority of the problems he confronted where quite insoluble, any-
> how in the short run, so it was probably a good thing to try to get the
> parties together on the basis of some complicated formula that none of
> them properly understood. . . . But this may have been for quite another
> reason. For Hammarskjöld had more charm than most, and a strong desire
> to please.[29]

The secretary-general possesses no hard material power. Rather, he represents a quintessence, the "abstraction of the international community."[30] It is
thus that he can justifiably be viewed as a voice, speaking out moral principles
on the international stage and desires to please.[31] Nevertheless, the various
efforts and diplomatic actions of the secretary-general can have consider-
able influence on political outcomes. Secretaries-general are aware that their
power to shape political discourse and outcomes can suddenly disappear.
The constraint of power on authorities is also evident in the agency of the
secretary-general who can find innovative ways in blocked situations such
as Hammarskjöld did. Just like Hannah Arendt's emphasis upon the "legiti-
macy of power," Hammarskjöld holds in *Markings*, that "only he deserves
power who every day justifies it."[32]

The Legacy of Hammarskjöld

Hammarskjöld was an old-style, some would say aristocratic, diplomat, keen
not to force issues, knowing how the rules of the game work.[33] He saw the UN

as a "means to an end, and not an end in itself [that] might be superseded."[34] The UN is a "venture in progress towards an international community living in peace under the laws of justice."[35]

Similarly, Herbert Butterfield put forward an idea of diplomacy as way of civilizing influence: "A system of diplomacy incorporating the virtues of charity and self-restraint constituted an element of civilization which made it easier for people to be good in their relations with those whom they saw as others, outside their own society or community of shared rules, understandings and outlook."[36] For Butterfield, diplomacy lies at the heart of international relations. Paul Sharp captures Butterfield's understanding of diplomacy in two basic propositions. First, one must acknowledge "the differences, rather than the similarities, between ourselves and those who are distant from us in either time or space." Second, "people's understandings of their own circumstances are necessarily incomplete and wilfully partial, especially in their disputes with one another."[37] Third, as Butterfield himself argues, "we shall find at the heart of everything a kernel of difficulty which is essentially a problem of diplomacy as such."[38]

Some scholars and activists argue that the UN is a Christian (and thus Western) organization. The argument therefore is that the discourse on peace, a Christian legacy, rather than the one of justice, is predominant—whereas Islam and Judaism discourses appear more concerned with justice and are not adequately represented in the UN.[39] Still, the gravity supporting, for example, Catholic social teaching is its aim toward social justice. Justice is thus not least part of a Christian discourse. Moreover, in Catholic teaching there is "no peace without justice."[40] Two years after Hammarskjöld's death, Pope John Paul's encyclical *Pacem in Terris* linked the quest for peace to human rights and the pursuit of justice, addressing all people, not merely Catholics. In the light of Hammarskjöld's ethical framework, this Catholic concern of the interdependence between peace and justice reflects his concerns to bridge the gap between the notions of the UN as an organization dominated by the discourse of peace at the expense of justice.

Hammarskjöld's quest for the UN was not least to establish a political philosophy of the organization. He realistically acknowledged the fact that the nation state was the "highest fully organized form of life of peoples."[41] He accepted that the UN was dependent on the will of its members, particularly the permanent ones in the Security Council. At the same time, however, he saw the organization as a new element in international affairs, especially due to its principles anchored in the Charter like justice and equal political and economic opportunities. His view was that "a reliable and just world order could only be built pragmatically by making precedents and by case law."[42] Hammarskjöld's notion of international affairs was one of focusing on the international society (the primacy of nation states) rather than on world society (the primacy of individuals). Nevertheless, he and his legacy were on the *way* "from international to world society." International society mainly "is about the institutionalisation of shared interest and identity amongst states, and puts the creation and maintenance of shared norms, rules and institutions . . . having constitutive rather than merely instrumental implications."[43]

Hammarskjöld was convinced that the UN was a new element in international affairs. It is thus not surprising that Hammarskjöld thought of the secretary-general as a "secular pope."[44] His efforts while in office put "transcendence of the states-system at the centre of IR theory," which "does not rest on an ontology of states" but focuses on "global societal identities and arrangements."[45] At the same time, Hammarskjöld was aware that any society in international affairs does not entirely relies on individuals. The secretary-general was, as his successors still are, in other words, indeed a part of the global elite. This is particularly because the rules of conduct and political and diplomatic innovation are made, to a large degree, by this very global elite.[46]

Hammarskjöld's political and diplomatic innovations have been the introduction of the so-called quiet or private diplomacy, preventive diplomacy, and the UN presence in conflict areas (the so-called blue-helmet missions).[47] Understanding the UN and particularly the secretary-general as a front line of a moral force, Hammarskjöld focused on preventive diplomacy.[48] In 1955, for example, he obtained the release of American aviators imprisoned in the Peoples Republic of China by extensive silent diplomacy. *Markings* reflects this experience:

> He broke fresh ground—because, and only because, he had the courage to
> go ahead without asking whether other were following or even understood
> . . . he had been granted a faith which required no confirmation—a contact
> with reality, light and intense like the touch of a loving hand: a union in
> self-surrender without destruction, where his heart was lucid and his mind
> loving.[49]

Although Hammarskjöld viewed the UN also in an idealistic manner, he remained realistic in his actions. He saw the UN as "a symbol of ideas, and … an attempt to translate into action a faith—the faith which one inspired a Beethoven … to his great profession of freedom, the brotherhood of man. And a world of harmony."[50] It may be this very notion, which comes close to a characterization of a religious institution, that persuaded Hammarskjöld in his belief of the necessity of the UN. In a certain sense, it can justifiably be described, "in essence [not in language as] a religious institution."[51] On a UN concert day, Hammarskjöld described analogies to the task of the UN along Beethoven's ninth Symphony:

> On this road from conflict and emotion to reconciliation in this final hymn of praise, Beethoven has given us a confession and a credo which we, who work within and for this Organization, may well make our own. We take part in the continuous fight between conflicting interests and ideologies which so far has marked the history of mankind, but we may never lose our faith that the first movements one day will be followed by the fourth movement. In that faith we strive to bring order and purity into chaos and anarchy. Inspired by that faith we try to impose the laws of the human mind and of the integrity of the human will on the dramatic evolution in which we are all engaged and in which we all carry our responsibility.[52]

As Kurt Waldheim, one of his successors, put it, "Hammarskjöld did not, I think, regard the secretary-general primarily as 'force' in world politics but rather as an honest broker, a catalyst, and someone to whom governments could go for help in critical situations."[53] Hammarskjöld's diplomatic actions were characterized by his realistic face-saving approach.[54] Realism stresses that international actors should avoid situations where they cannot pull themselves out without losing face. Due to his idea of diplomacy, Hammarskjöld engaged in multilateral diplomacy through which he sought to transcript the world toward a world society not overridden by "sovereign national states in armed competition."[55] Hammarskjöld's view of the UN was thus not a structural or mechanical one—of which the foremost task is applying pressure or maintaining a balance—but rather a process-oriented one. Just as he interpreted his position as secretary-general, Hammarskjöld believed that the organization of the "United Nations stands outside—necessarily outside—all confessions but it is, nevertheless, an instrument of faith."[56] This is also obvious in *Markings*: "Dare he, for whom circumstances make it possible to realize his true destiny, refuse it simply because he is not prepared to give up everything else?"[57] To say yes and to leave everything behind was his approach to the position of the secretary-general, understood as an international civil servant as he outlined it at a lecture delivered at Oxford University in 1961:

> The international civil servant must keep himself under strictest observation. He is not requested to be a neuter in the sense that he has to have no sympathies or antipathies, that there are to be no interest which are close to him in personal capacity or that he is to have no ideas or ideals that matter for him. However, he is requested to be fully aware of those human reactions and meticulously check himself so that they are not permitted to influence his actions. . . . If the international civil servant knows himself to be free from such personal influences in his actions and guided solely by the common aims and rules laid down for, and by the Organization he serves and by recognized legal principles, then he has done his duty . . . this is a question of integrity, and if integrity in the sense of respect for law and respect for the truth were to drive him into positions of conflict with this or that interest, then that conflict is a sign of his neutrality and not of his failure to observe neutrality—then it is in line, not in conflict, with his duties as an international civil servant.[58]

His statement before the Security Council in the course of the Suez Canal crisis 1956 further testifies to his commitment to international justice and peace, bound by the attempt of pursuing international justice. Moreover, the statement illustrates Hammarskjöld's image of the world organization and its secretary-general:

> The principles of the Charter are, by far, greater than the Organization in which they are embodied, and the aims which they are to safeguard are holier than the policies of any single nation or people. As a servant of the Organization, the Secretary-General has the duty to maintain his usefulness by avoiding public stands on conflicts between Member Nations unless

and until such an action might help to resolve the conflict. However, the discretion and impartiality required of the Secretary-General cannot serve of any other assumption than that within the necessary limits of human frailty and honest differences of opinion—all Member nations honour their pledge to observe all Articles of the Charter . . . Where the Members to consider that another view of the duties of the Secretary-General than the one here stated would better serve the interests of the Organization, it is their obvious right to act accordingly.[59]

The Other and Positive Mimesis

Hammarskjöld remained neutral in his political efforts and a mystic in private life. His "value system, which upheld public service guided by morality, found a firm footing in the role of international servant."[60] The outstanding insight about this posthumous Nobel Peace Prize winner is that his political actions were not least guided by his mystical worldview. He saw his belief not as a kind of request for inner immigration, but rather as a demand to act according to his belief. This is most obvious while having a closer look at the civic component of his ethical framework, which "was his personal sacrifice to public service."[61] This "personal sacrifice to public service" illustrates the importance of personal qualities and virtues of the office holders.

> Often it was the personal qualities and persistence of the secretary-general that were the key to successful implementation of the chosen means. . . . Good faith, honesty, truth telling—all the old-fashioned virtues—can become tools of peacemaking in the hands of the secretaries-general, especially if they are perceived as using those qualities in the service of some greater good.[62]

Like Buber, Hammarskjöld shared the emphasis of the attitudes toward the Other, reflecting "the tension between realism and idealism and exclusiveness versus inclusiveness."[63] This tension is mirrored in Hammarskjöld's efforts as he optimistically acknowledged the UN as an idealistic enterprise but, at the same time, was aware of its realistic constraints. His conception comes close to the concept of Emanuel Levinas who developed a thought in which there is no allergy to otherness. At the same time he [Levinas] realistically appreciated the modern state. He recognized that ethics demand politics but situated ethics above politics. His nuanced position is both realistic, taking into account human violence, and normative in describing a person's infinite responsibility. His thought combines the call of the other with a realistic approach that also guarantees the rights of the same.[64]

It becomes clear that Hammarskjöld saw the UN, and particularly the principles of the Charter, as the way to reconcile the differences of single nation states. "The Charter was the foundation stone of his public self, as his religious faith was the foundation stone for the private man."[65] Hammarskjöld, like every other secretary-general, had to balance different interests and values: interests between the UN members and personal values. The ideal secretary-general might thus as well be a normative negotiator seeking balance while considering the international body as a collection of possibilities confronting various evils.[66]

For mimetic theory, "evil" refers to the mimetic desire that René Girard accounts for as the source of violence.[67] For Girard, as illustrated previously, mimetic rivalry is the main cause of interpersonal violence. We always imitate what we admire.[68] Hammarskjöld acknowledged this insight into mimetic rivalry in his thoughts about Lucifer in *Markings*: "It was when Lucifer first congratulated himself upon his angelic behavior that he became the tool of evil."[69] Yet in his writings, we find illustrations of positive mimesis, founded in mysticism.

Because God is a personal God, "a vision in which God *is*," as Hammarskjöld put it in *Markings*, what counts is the inner life.[70] The introspective abilities, which he admired, illustrate how peace is its highest implementation and realization of being. It is thus, as Miroslav Volf argues, that peace can only be achieved by an appeal for the practice of (social and political) reconciliation that reflects the love of God.[71] Religion therefore cannot be distinguished from the political sphere. Eric Voegelin acknowledged this by recognizing if the political community loses its *summum bonum*—an orientation toward the transcendental instead of a *summum malum*—only passionate fear for a violent death will control human action and ends in aggressive overcoming of the Other.[72] Hammarskjöld acknowledged this in his mystic ethical framework. Not surprisingly, he thought about the understanding of Original Sin and of how to overcome it in a living relation with God:

> We can reach the point where it becomes possible for us to recognize and understand Original Sin, that dark counter-center of evil in our nature—that is to say, though it *is* not our nature, it is *of* it—that something within us which rejoices when disaster befalls the very cause we are trying to serve, or misfortune overtakes even those whom we love. Life in God is not an escape from this, but the way to gain full insight concerning it. It is not our depravity which forces a fictitious religious explanation upon us, but the experience of religious reality which forces the "Night Side" out into the light. It is when we stand in the righteous all-seeing light of love that we can dare to look at, admit, and *consciously* suffer under this something in us which wills disaster, misfortune, defeat to everything outside the sphere of our narrowest self-interest. So in a living relation to God it is the necessary precondition for the self-knowledge which enables us to follow a straight path, and so be victorious over ourselves, forgiven by ourselves.[73]

In relating to Christian mystics, particularly in the tradition of the *Imitatio Christi*, Hammarskjöld, the secular pope was unknowingly well aware of positive mimesis's force to overcome human conditioned violence through relating oneself toward Christ. He is thus an example how faith can influence political structures in international affairs—in this case, even the world organization UN. It is thus in fact "possible to generalize that Hammarskjöld's ethical framework also influenced both his international political agenda and his method of administration." At the same time, it is important to note that Hammarskjöld's "ethical framework never revealed itself as a public crusade."[74] According to O'Brien, "Hammarskjöld, more than anyone else, gave the UN a focus of moral authority that would attract an international loyalty, and used it in the cause of peace and justice."[75] His emphasis toward the Other can be understood as the secretary-general's understanding of God's fraternalism. His life and legacy give a positive answer to the question of whether we are "willing to innovate with and politicise discourses that reflect on the spiritual dimension of Otherness and its value in knowing the Self?"[76]

Having illustrated Hammarskjöld's ethical framework, his main thought in *Markings* is obvious. One has to let his ego—and thus the negative mimesis—go and act as an instrument of God: "Not I, but God in me!," as he puts it in *Markings*.[77] He was certain that his task would lead to the ultimate sacrifice. As he put in *Markings*, it is the responsibility for, not to, God that is essentially telling oneself: "If you fail, it is God, thanks to your having betrayed Him, who will fail mankind. You fancy you can be responsible *to* God: can you carry the responsibility *for* God?"[78] It is thus certainly no coincidence that he took up the responsibility *for* a political community, the UN, and consequently perceiving it as an instrument of faith in saying yes to oneself, to God, and to every fate one may face. Hammarskjöld's statements during the Cold War illustrate his struggle between "I" and "you" in the interpersonal sphere. Hammarskjöld is, in the words of Rowan Williams, a

> picture of an adult politician in a not very adult world. One could say that he expected too much of professional politicians and all those whose job it was to defend local interests. But he offered a perspective without which all politics is empty. His work and words declare that it is possible to see the world with what could best be called creative detachment, and without self-pity.[79]

Conclusion

The international civil servant Hammarskjöld united mystics and realistic diplomatic engagement in a unique manner because he amalgamated his personal convictions and the spirit of the Charter of the UN, knowing that the destructive powers of the world are here to stay as both Realism and mimetic theory point out. It is thus not surprising that the two books he constantly kept with him were the Charter of the UN and the Psalms. His concerns are echoed in the question verbalized by Herbert Butterfield: "All we can ask—while the military force heaps itself up around us—is the question: Can the world be made more tolerable in spite of this power which solidifies in great masses amongst nations and empires?"[80] Toward this end, the United Nations, in the words of Hammarskjöld, "was not created to bring us to heaven but to save us from hell."[81] However, the insights of both mimetic theory and classical Realism help to figure out how to stay on that road. Because of its awareness of humans drive to mimesis, both stress that politics is an interplay between principles and contingent facts. In practice, as Hammarskjöld's legacy illustrates, that means that politics is more art than engineering.[82]

5.

Toward Competition
without Violence

---

ife and politics are about "competition without shooting each other,"
Harry S. Truman reflected in his memoirs, which I used as a starting
point in the preface.[1] Similarly, Hans Morgenthau argued, "the crude
methods of personal combat have been replaced by the refined instruments
of social, commercial, and professional competition."[2] We live in a violent
world; there is no question about that. However, it likely has always been
this way. Realism and mimetic theory were always clear about that. Violence
remains a part of social and political conduct. "Ideals are peaceful, history
is violent."[3] Politics is about taming this competitive and eventually violent
state of political conduct. Ideals, however, often rely on violent means to
bring the promised peace—that is why "history is violent." The introduction
of the Leviathan in Thomas Hobbes's war of all against all, for example, led
to a war of all against one.[4]

History shows that it is insufficient to assume any kind of a rational
social contract as the basis for society. Disorder is the normal state, order the
exception that constantly needs to be proved and explained. Much of disorder
and violence is due to sameness not difference between people, as mimetic
theory points out.[5] This is, however, not only true for liberal-style democracy.
Extremists also take on to egalitarian ideas to enlist and empower followers.

Scott Atran concluded that "Jihad" is in fact "an egalitarian, equal-opportunity employer."[6] Globalization propels the very existence of cultural diversity and the awareness of it. Religious traditions, as it turns out, are well aware of this insight. So were political leaders and diplomats like Hammarskjöld and George Kennan. When asked to witness about the character of his colleague Robert Oppenheimer on a security clearance hearing, Kennan stated:

> I think the church has known that. Had the church applied to St. Francis the criteria for relating solely to his youth it would not have been able for him to be what he was later . . . It is only the great sinners who become the great saints and in the life of the Government there can be applied this analogy.[7]

At the same time, as argued earlier, global culture increases the likelihood that this will generate rivalry, competition, and conflict.[8] As we are all the same, we all long mimetically for the same goods. Those goods are chiefly not the fantastic and unreachable ones but the very closest ones. It is when we enter into a dialogue and pursue power that the political gets its shape in the degree of intensity of the connection between subjects and objects. What is true for interpersonal relations, as Girard's anthropological theory holds, is also true for international politics as Morgenthau acknowledged.[9] From this perspective, it is logical for Realism to tie power and politics into one single term.[10]

Throughout this book, I make no distinction between structural violence and other forms of violence such as the actual use of force.[11] The basic assumptions of Realism and mimetic theory alike forbid such a sharp differentiation. The political has no fixed interest. "Its limits lie only in the confrontation between divergent wills, interests, and the forms of power they can wield."[12] Realism is thus foremost a tool of political judgment, mixing positive and normative theory.[13] For classical Realism, international politics is and remains uncertain, contingent, and consequential. Hence, what matters is that people seek more than just power and security.[14]

The Realist principle of the desire for power, emphasizing agency, translates in social life into lust and consequently the struggle for power. In international politics, this reflects itself in the politics of the status quo, of imperialism, or of prestige.[15] There is thus no difference between domestic and international politics. Politics, ultimately, for Realism derives from individuals. Morgenthau conceded that there is no escape from the desire for power in any kind of politics. However, there are ways that it can be tamed via ritualization.[16] The often invoked but assumedly materialist principle of the balance of power is thus in fact a societal and actual social phenomenon.[17] Realism is well aware of the need for checks and balances, as the human drive for power is one that will not be satisfied by survival and securitization.[18]

We Ourselves—the Desire for Recognition, Status, and Revenge

To desire what is recognized as a standard proceeding is logical. It is thus that many so-called Third World states suffer from an internal lack of positive role models to imitate. For example, the foreign policy of the Islamic Republic of Iran, since the Revolution in 1979, can be explained in considering two intertwined factors: the ideology of Islamism as a kind of countering the "evilness" of modernity as represented by the West, and a distinct Third World ideology as can be seen in the rhetoric of the former Non-Aligned Movement. The regime cannot appreciate the engagement (i.e., in offering civil nuclear facilities) of the West, since this would mean to lose the concept of the enemy. The desire to gain such (nuclear) power arises because the West generates these weapons of its own power. It is therefore not a desire simply to copy the West but to follow what others desire, like the will for (nuclear) power.

Other examples include South Africa and Ukraine. After various changes (different leaders and group thinking; regime change or different costs; changing geopolitical factors of the end of the Cold War) South Africa gave up its nuclear weapons program.[19] Although it eventually did so in the mid-1990s, the newly independent nation of Ukraine in 1991 immediately was on the lookout for a different role model and found it in the politics of the West. William Wallace reports of a seminar in 1991, provided by Harvard University to the government of Ukraine:

> It was attended by a dozen ministers, including the ministers of foreign affairs and economics, a number of military and civilian officials, and

members of the Ukrainian Parliament. Many had never been abroad; MPs from Rukh had never previously met anyone from outside the USSR. They knew almost nothing of the basic rules and assumptions of the international society of which they claimed membership; the foreign minister's opening statement declared the "basic aims" of Ukrainian foreign policy to be full membership of NATO and the EC by the end of 1993.[20]

Next to the obvious mimetic statement of the government's will to join NATO and the EC is the introduction of the reporting author that makes clear that international politics is also about the rules of the games (e.g., diplomacy). They make international politics (i.e., the desire for power) what they are, and that practice, in the first place, actually makes international society (i.e., the taming, the ordering of the former).[21] What mimetic theory reminds us of is that in our enlightened age we are either not used to it anymore or, and indeed more often, we consciously veil violence and let it work unconsciously. Western politicians readily decry the use of violence as a means of politics, as we can see at the condemnation of Russia's foreign policy concerning Ukraine and in many other instances. At the same time, however, it causes surprise that the Western (i.e., mainly the U.S.) way of conducting foreign policy in the twentieth and twenty-first centuries produces so much anger and resentments across the world, leading to questions such as why the "rest" hates us?[22]

One reason is that this kind of foreign policy is not guided by political ends but primarily by military means pursued by interventionism for the sake of global dominance.[23] Another warrant leading to this conclusion is the ever-growing use of violent means as self-defense. The offensive-defensive distinction becomes blurred ever more in relying on prevention in order of proclaimed self-defense.[24] Seen from the perspective of mimetic theory, John Mearsheimer's thesis that the crisis in Ukraine is also the fault of the West seems appealing.[25] The external promotion of human rights, the European Union's and NATO's eastern outreach, and actual enlargement conflicted with Russia's interest in the region. Far from being the only reason, these promotions as well fueled the rivalry between East and West. One of the main ingredients of the success of the United States as a superpower is, according to Henry Kissinger, its practice of the "cultivation of shared principles."[26] In other words, the United States tried to achieve peace throughout the world via spreading the democratic principle, thereby generating itself as a role model.

The end of the Cold War, the beginning of which was in Truman's tenure, and its rival visions of world order were once thought to be the beginning of a new world order. What happened instead was that scholars and the public found themselves bewildered by the surge of aggression marked by civil wars, terrorism, and power politics. After years of an assumedly reasonable relationship between East and West, Russia's military intervention in Ukraine and Syria took scholars of peace by surprise.[27] The former U.S. secretary of state John Kerry, for example, remarked on that occasion, "You just don't in the 21st century behave in 19th century fashion by invading another country on completely trumped up pre-text."[28]

Other puzzling features of international politics include the outcomes of the Arab Spring. As the events unfolded, the revolutions were supposedly the unleashing of public energy longing for freedom. Instead, the events shocked scholars over their religious context and violent fallouts. Facing continuous conflict in the Middle East and other regions, we are struggling to understand the sweeping success of the Islamic State, even more so to find a moral vocabulary for its brutality. Most often, this practice aims to achieve a state, as various political movements from the IRA to the Kurds to the Islamic State illustrate. However, it is not just "we ourselves."[29] A state seeks recognition from the international community. This was the case for most political movements that achieved or struggled to achieve a state.

The desire to play along with the rules of the game of the international remains the rule to which most actors stick. The Islamic State's lack of interest for recognition on the international stage as a legitimate entity of international relations is the exception. Even the Taliban opened an embassy in Qatar.[30] The beheading of U.S. and UK journalists, made publicly available by the Islamic State in 2014, not least served as a legitimation for intervention.[31] The reaction around the world thereupon is illustrative for the significance of mimetic theory's most basic foundational principles: sacrifice and victimhood, illustrating that politics inevitable rests on individualization.

The Individualization of Politics and Responsibility

International politics become more and more individualized and international society became one to hold not states but individuals accountable. The former taboo of the assassination of political leaders slowly vanishes.[32] The war against terrorism is illustrative for this development: the killing of individuals with the objective to seek revenge and justice, legitimized by rules that are grounded in the belief of moral progress via legalization.[33] On the other side, beheadings of individuals, distributed via social media, led to an increase of the intensity of the U.S. and other states' military engagements against the Islamic State. The growing awareness of cruelty around the world pushes great powers to act.

Classical, twentieth-century Realists understood this dilemma while they crafted the analytical concept of the "national interest," which is neither objective nor fixed. The national interest is rather a corrective at which the exercise of power must measure itself.[34] Morgenthau's phrase "lust for power" comes close to Girard's reflection on desire. We live in an age of a growing excess of individual accountability and responsibility.[35] International politics often pursues justice by bringing individuals before the International Criminal Court.[36] This is not surprising, as a judicial system subsidizes the mimetic desire for revenge and sacrifice. The judicial system in domestic and international politics alike replace sacrifice in order to keep peace. However, the logic of sacrifice persists where the judicial system has no stronghold.[37]

Mimetic theory and Realism illustrate that violence does not prevail only among societies but primarily within them. Individual accountability, a trend that began with the Nuremberg War Trials in the aftermath of the Second World War, is an epiphany of veiled violence. Although not explicitly acknowledged, the scapegoat mechanism is what keeps societies together. Crimes, also in the international realm, largely attributed to individuals and courts are perceived as an important and appropriate measure to engage with this belief. International criminal law holds that "responsibility for war crimes rests with individuals."[38] This "excess of responsibility" is based on the comforting myth that few people are responsible and the deception that other causes of violence are obsolete, for example structural causes.[39] The judicial system, seen in the light of mimetic theory, is an institution to replace sacrifice and to keep peace. Where it has no hold, the logic of sacrifice persists.[40]

However, not only events far away from enlightened Western academia call for a Realist mimetic lens to understand them. Recall, for instance, Margaret Thatcher's statement on TINA (there is no alternative) regarding the world financial crisis. Germany's chancellor Angela Merkel made a similar remark stating that the financial aid for Greece was without alternatives. Reducing policy and politics to but one choice is certainly a dangerous drive of current world affairs. Recall the reactions of the various uprisings from Libya to Syria. Policy makers and scholars argue that there is no alternative to a humanitarian intervention.[41] Such calls, however morally justified as they may be, most often only give short- or at least middle-range advice.[42] Moreover, they do not recognize that restrained actions such as no-kill zones never can remain genuinely defensive and thus not as minimalist as they claim to be.[43]

While mimetic theory and Realism focus on order and disorder, disorder is paramount. "The refusal to recognize the primitive symbolic character of modern conflict, the radical un-modernity of our warfare is one of the most dangerous illusions of our time," writes former archbishop of Canterbury, Rowan Williams[44] There is an obvious link between the natural state of disorder and the fabricated nature of order, just as the judicial system illustrates. Acknowledging this fact of social and political life, the Realist tradition was primarily concerned with order as a moral problem rather than an instrumental problem.[45] This is also evident when we have a look at the political problems caused by urbanization.

Urbanization and the Politics of Resentment

Empirical research shows that population growth, which results in increased density in urban space, can increase the likeliness of conflict, thus potentially becoming a driving force of the political's existential logic.[46] This is not to say that there is a causal link between urban density and violence.[47] Nonetheless, the very existence of the potential of the political's existential logic illustrates that the density accompanying urbanization exceeds authorities and residents responding to it.[48] Density, according to Colin McFarlane, is at "once a topographical" problem and a "problem of topological politics of space."[49] Urban uprisings are increasing on a global scale.[50] The Arab Spring, for example, was partly motivated by the access of youth to social media, which made them aware of Western lifestyles in other parts of the world, buying into a "justice-based international order."[51] Urbanization, in this regard, serves as an equalizing force that makes people aware of what others have. As such, urbanization contributes in various ways to the generalization of the international realm, where complexity and diversity are acknowledged and dealt with politically.[52]

Finding and defining identity is more difficult where there is less difference between people, such as in dense urban areas. Since the end of the Cold War, cities have made the coexistence of many diverse identities possible.[53] But as Pierre Bourdieu observed, "Social identity lies in difference, and difference is asserted against what is closest, which represents the greatest threat."[54] The point here is not that identities have to clash to emerge and shape in a violent manner, rather that the vanishing of differences may lead to greater potential for future conflict facing a growing globalization.[55] In terms of mimetic theory, this means sameness, not difference, is the problem in political interaction. Rivalry indeed emerges from relative rather than absolute disadvantage.[56] Social, political, and economic inequalities do not lead to violence per se. Given the increasing possibilities of comparison between individuals, there is certainly a potential danger of the outbreak of violence. Mimetic theory points to the danger of comparison, and Morgenthau's concept of the political assumed the individual's struggle for the "position among his fellows" as a condition for the contestation over power, which characterizes the political.[57]

In a world that becomes flat, where physical distance is less of an issue, humans tend to compare their lifestyles with others and imitate each other's material and nonmaterial desire.[58] The democratic dogma of egalitarianism potentially pushes rivalry to its edges, based on wholesaling the possibility to imitate the desire of others.[59] Globalization's homogenization efforts led to a globalized "Jihad" on the one side and a globalized "McWorld" on the other side, both propelled by the globalization of resentment.[60] Peer-group comparison, an awareness of what others have and want, is one reason why growing economic wealth, pressed by globalization, goes hand in hand with strong sentiments of nationalism.[61] The more options there are to imitate, the more likely it is that people struggle over the options available. Urbanization, seen from the angle of demographic development and leading to partial improvement of social and economic conditions for some, raises the stakes of rivalry over relative gains for others.

The relative deprivation of basic living conditions drives the "gap between what people feel rightfully entitled to and what they are capable of achieving under existing circumstances."[62] Eventually the long-fueled outbreak of desiring what others desire, often disguised as nationalism, serves as a condition of civic conflict in the urban sphere. For example, research on political conflict in sub-Saharan and Asian cities points out that urban social disorder is associated with low economic growth and hybrid democratic regimes.[63] An early study on urbanization and world politics concluded that most worries about political order and social wellbeing in the context of "rapid urban growth and underemployment [are] *political* rather than economic."[64] Civic conflict is "directly related to the urban realm in that it generally takes place *in* cities and it is linked to the socioeconomic and spatial particularities of cities."[65] While civil conflict is "essentially instrumental, civic conflict is generally expressive and . . . falls short of taking control of formal structures of power."[66] In other words, security becomes urbanized.[67] Saskia Sassen describes this expressive character of civic conflict as the complexity of powerlessness.[68] The protest movements during the Arab Spring and other urban uprisings may have had no power in a material sense, but they still were political via their presence on city streets and squares. One reason why civic conflict is globally on the rise is that it "is a common *response* to that rapid urbanisation."[69]

Violence and disorder within groups are persistent components of political conduct. Paradoxically, however, scholars of political theory and international studies became concerned with a notion of the political that aligned with a desire for order, despite the fact that disorder and violence remain the offspring of political entities.[70] As James Scott concludes in his study of the state, the "enlightenment belief in the self-improvement of men became, by degrees, a belief in the perfectibility of social order."[71] An apparent example of this belief in the self-improvement of men can be seen in city planning that fails to account for the subjectivity of those living there.[72] This is obvious in the conditions of the suburbs in the northern hemisphere, planned at the drawing board, illustrative for a mechanistic urban policy. The

Banlieues of Paris are only the most prominent examples, eventually declared
to be counter excavations in the search for nonpolitical instruments to solve
political urban problems.[73]

Urbanization in the Global North set in after there was a consolidated
state in place, one that did not promote civic conflict because it could not
provide the essential needs, security, and welfare for its citizens. Cities in the
Global North began to rise before the communication revolution, which
made the rest of the world aware of Western materialism.[74] What is more, the
urban space as an economic hub once tended to solve conflicts by economizing them via material tradeoffs. Today, this intervening economizing action
of the urban is challenged around the globe. Cities no longer only mitigate
conflict. It is more likely that structural challenges of civic and civil order
make cities breed conflict themselves.[75] The urbanizing international realm,
however, also illustrates the relational carvings of the political, showing that
the political signifies only the possibility, not necessity, of violence.

Conclusion

Mimetic theory argues that desire is not merely socially constructed. Doing
so questions mainstream assumptions of the rational autonomy of the individual and spontaneous desire.[76] The Realist revival in international political
philosophy, I argue, is not least that persistent because of the traditional Realist claim that there is no use of a clear-cut distinction between descriptive
and prescriptive theory.[77] This is because politics cannot be split up between
how we think about living together and how we actually do so. As Realism
and mimetic theory illustrate, we are not completely free and autonomous
to choose the way we conduct social and thus political affairs. If this were the
case, there would be no need for the study of International Relations once
survival is secured. Forces beyond cost-benefit analysis and the satisfying of
basic human needs ultimately drive politics. Although Morgenthau's conception of the political "depends on circumstances of time and place and does
not result from a ground of principle," there are circumstances of time and
place such as the desire for power and recognition that remain the same.[78]

Mimetic theory provides insights to the interplay of the evolving and
nature of power. This attaches mimetic theory with Realism's assumptions

about norms, ethics, and morality in politics. Mimetic theory itself points toward the dangers of egalitarian approaches and reflects instead on tradition-dependent mindful virtues. Realism does so as well, pointing to the virtue of prudence of political leaders. It is thus that I make the "case for a classical approach," as Hedley Bull called it.[79] International theory is more of a practical philosophy.[80] In the words of Martin Wight, "international theory is the political philosophy of international relations."[81]

Certainly, there is no one-size-fits-all approach to explain or even understand international politics via such a conceptualization of Realism. Although Girard himself and some of his students might evoke this assumption, I do not. This does not mean that International Relations scholars were not able to point to the dangers of violence provoked by mimetic desire. International Relations, while looking at anthropological theories like mimetic theory, must bet "on the education of humanity, even if he is not sure he will win his wager," in the words of Raymond Aron.[82]

The discussion I try to initiate between mimetic theory and Realism helps International Relations pursuing a better understanding of its theoretical claims and actual politics. That remains true, even if an appreciation of Girard's thoughts can only help International Relations to make implicit claims and theoretical assumptions of Realism more explicit. This is, for example, the case in turning to a Realist view on reconciliation. It reminds us that politics is not only about the last questions of how a perfect society would or should look like. Rather, it is about the day-to-day practice of living a good life despite all compromises one might have to make. Mimetic theory shows that there are fewer differences among humans then we wish. What is more, mimetic theory leads to the conclusion—particularly when looking at "successful" reconciliation—that the consequence must be to strictly refuse violence.[83] Mimetic theory, seen with the lens of classical Realism, illustrates the uselessness of attempts that rely on political and juristically processes primarily on finding individual accountability and responsibility. The continuation of the war on terrorism, largely waged with special operations and targeted killing practices, only accelerated this trend in doing away with reciprocity in warfare.[84] Yet still, even

> if the mimetic nature of human desire is responsible for most of the violent acts and distresses us, we should not conclude that mimetic desire is bad in

itself. If our desires were not mimetic, they would be forever fixed on pre-determined objects; they would be a particular form of instinct. Human beings could no more change their desire than cows their appetite for grass. Without mimetic desire there would be neither freedom nor humanity. Mimetic desire is intrinsically good.[85]

Dag Hammarskjöld illustrates why mimetic desire is intrinsically good. The UN secretary-general was able to play out character traits of mysticism and realistic diplomatic assessment and engagement. He was able to do so because he amalgamated his personal convictions, which never have been static, and the spirit of the UN Charter. In his own words, "The United Nations was not created to bring us to heaven but to save us from hell."[86] With his emphasis toward the Other, Hammarskjöld's life and legacy gives a positive answer to the question of whether we are "willing to innovate with and politicise discourses that reflect on the spiritual dimension of Otherness and its value in knowing the Self?"[87] Hammarskjöld, as Rowan Williams contemplated, "recognized that public office is not about anxiously conserving status or winning arguments. He was sharply aware of the shadows in his own motivation, and confronted them patiently and remorselessly in his private writing."[88]

The desire for recognition, the power of mimetic behavior and its implications, such as the fading distinction between normative and positive theory, does have a real impact in international affairs. I outlined this with several examples, from individual agency to questions of international society, the international system, and specific practices. It turns out that not only the mechanisms of mimetic desire and its taming instruments provide ample potential to understand international politics more comprehensively, but also that the very reason of mimetic desire is a major afterburner in international political conduct. This is contradictory to many normative assumptions about international politics, for example the fact that global inequality rises. However, mimetic desire does not only, maybe not even primarily, orient itself at material objects. The possibility of an awareness of what others desire is not limited to access to material wealth. Simply being aware of what others desire is where it all starts. This might mean being aware of what celebrities desire, but more often than not, it means being aware of what our neighbor desires. The less distance there is, the more complicated it gets to find a distinction. International politics, after all, affects our daily life just because it also is about daily life around the world.

The struggle for power among nations that Morgenthau had in mind and that became synonymous for the Realist family of thought is also based on the struggle for the imitation and desire among nations, becoming fixed on the other until finally scapegoating it. Indicating assumptions of mimetic theory, human's desire for power is a continuum in Morgenthau's work.[89] Seen from the Realist perspective, seeking absolute gains such as the global common good by assumedly universal notions of justice and freedom is not a practice in politics.[90] Perceived from this angle, I take a renewed look at the discussion of relative and absolute gains in International Relations theory.[91] If at all, relative gains matter for Realism. Throughout the book, I illustrate that this focus on relative gains is one that classical Realism and mimetic theory share.

I acknowledge the problematic equalization of human desire and the desire of political actors such as states. Such equalizations are persistently in danger of drifting into a perception of methodological individualism. Nonetheless, what is desired is a result of imitating others. In the "human conduct in a world of states," it is unlikely that one state would or even could exclude itself from the framework of conducting politics in the mainstream way.[92] It may be therefore, as Alexander Wendt argued, that in an arena where everything is contested, the common denominator is to say that states are actors or "persons," attributing them properties and qualities such as rationality, identities, interests, and beliefs.[93] However, what constructivists miss is the recognition of the relation between the political nature of humans and the ensuing political conditions. The political nature is a struggle for power caused by the desire for power, constituting the condition of politics. It is therefore that politics, and even more so international politics, always have a tragic component hardwired into their conduct.[94] Political action is inherently contradictory, pending between self-constitution and meaning. Analyses ignoring the insights of Realism and mimetic theory are thus bound to fall short of the complexity of human nature, as Realism points out, and the complexity of the resulting political conditions, as pointed out by mimetic theory.[95]

Notes

FOREWORD

1. Ronald Inglehart, *Culture Shift in Advanced Society* (Princeton, NJ: Princeton University Press, 1990).

2. Richard Ned Lebow, *A Cultural Theory of International Relations* (Cambridge: Cambridge University Press, 2008).

3. Richard Ned Lebow, *Why Nations Fight: Past and Future Motives for War* (Cambridge: Cambridge University Press, 2010).

4. Irving L. Janis and Leon Mann, *Decision Making: A Psychological Analysis of Conflict, Choice, and Commitment* (New York: Free Press, 1977); Avner Offer, "Going to War in 1914: A Matter of Honour?," *Politics and Society* 23 (1995): 213–41; Lebow, *Cultural Theory of International Relations*; Felix Berenskoetter, "Friends, There Are No Friends? An Intimate Reframing of the International," *Millennium* 35, no. 2 (2007): 647–76.

5. Silviya Lechner and Mervyn Frost, *Practice Theory in International Relations* (Cambridge: Cambridge University Press, 2018).

PREFACE

1. Margaret Truman, *Where the Buck Stops: The Personal and Private Writings of Harry S. Truman* (New York: Warner Books, 1990), 202.

2. See also, for example, Peter Stork, "Human Rights: Controlling the Uncontrollable?,"

in *Violence, Desire, and the Sacred: Girard's Mimetic Theory Across the Disciplines*, ed. Scott Cowdell, Chris Fleming, and Joel Hodge (New York: Continuum, 2012), 206.

3. See, for example, Robert H. Frank, *Choosing the Right Pond: Human Behavior and the Quest for Status* (Oxford: Oxford University Press, 1986). Francis Fukuyama characterizes one of the major drivers for identity politics based on comparison and the demand for recognition. "One compares oneself not globally to some absolute standard of wealth, but relative to a local group that one deals with socially." Francis Fukuyama, *Identity: The Demand for Dignity and the Politics of Resentment* (New York: Farrar Straus and Giroux, 2018), 85.

4. René Girard, *Violence and the Sacred* (Baltimore: Johns Hopkins University Press, 1979), 49.

5. René Girard, *The Scapegoat* (Baltimore: Johns Hopkins University Press, 1986); Girard, *Violence and the Sacred*.

6. Gilbert Keith Chesterton, *Collected Works*, vol. 1: *Heretics, Orthodoxy, The Blatchford Controversies* (San Francisco: Ignatius, 1986), 327–28.

7. Girard, *The Scapegoat*; Girard, *Violence and the Sacred*. For a brief introduction to mimetic theory see "René Girard and Mimetic Theory," Imitatio, http://www.imitatio.org/brief-intro.

8. See, for example, Paul W. Kahn, *Sacred Violence: Torture, Terror, and Sovereignty* (Ann Arbor: University of Michigan Press, 2008).

9. See also Roberto Farneti, *Mimetic Politics: Dyadic Patterns in Global Politics* (East Lansing: Michigan State University Press, 2015).

10. Marysia Zalewski, "'All These Theories yet the Bodies Keep Piling Up': Theory, Theorists, Theorising," in *Positivism and Beyond*, ed. Steve Smith, Ken Booth, and Marysia Zalewski (Cambridge: Cambridge University Press, 1996).

11. T. A. Jacoby, "A Theory of Victimhood: Politics, Conflict and the Construction of Victim-Based Identity," *Millennium: Journal of International Studies* 43, no. 2 (2015): 521. See also James C. Davies, "Towards a Theory of Revolution," *American Sociological Review* 27, no. 1 (1962): 5–19; Ted R. Gurr, *Why Men Rebel* (Princeton, NJ: Princeton University Press, 1970).

12. See, for example, Elisabetta Brighi and Antonio Cerella, "An Alternative Vision of Politics and Violence: Introducing Mimetic Theory in International Studies," *Journal of International Political Theory* 11, no. 1 (2015): 3–25; Barbara Fuchs, *Mimesis and Empire: The New World, Islam, and European Identities* (Cambridge: Cambridge University Press, 2001); Scott M. Thomas, "Culture, Religion and Violence: Rene Girard's Mimetic Theory," *Millennium: Journal of International Studies* 43, no. 1 (2014): 308–27; Pierpaolo Antonello and Paul Gifford, eds., *Can We Survive Our Origins? Readings in René Girard's Theory of Violence and the Sacred* (East Lansing: Michigan State University Press, 2015); Harald Wydra, *Politics and the Sacred* (Cambridge: Cambridge University Press, 2015).

13. See, for example, Robert O. Keohane, "Big Questions in the Study of World Politics," in *The Oxford Handbook of International Relations*, ed. Christian Reus-Smit and Duncan Snidal (Oxford: Oxford University Press, 2010), 708–15. For a critical case study in this regard see, for example, Timothy Nunan, *Humanitarian Invasion: Global Development in Cold War Afghanistan* (Cambridge: Cambridge University Press, 2016). Nicholas Rengger, "Political Theory and International Relations: Promised Land or Exit from Eden?," *International Affairs* 76, no. 4 (2000): 755–70.

14. See, for example, Kyle Scott, "A Girardian Critique of the Liberal Democratic Peace Theory," *Contagion: Journal of Violence, Mimesis, and Culture* 15/16 (2008–2009): 45–62.

15. Rengger, "Political Theory and International Relations," 766.

16. Rengger, "Political Theory and International Relations," 766.

17. Hans J. Morgenthau, "Science of Peace: A Rationalist Utopia," *Social Research* 42, no. 1 (1975): 21.

18. "Charlie Hebdo and Fundamentalism," Duncan Reyburn (blog), January 3, 2016, http://duncanreyburn.blogspot.co.at/2016/01/charlie-hebdo-and-fundamentalism.html.

19. Martti Koskenniemi, *The Gentle Civilizer of Nations: The Rise and Fall of International Law, 1870–1960* (Cambridge: Cambridge University Press, 2002), 470.

20. Alison McQueen, "Political Realism and the Realist 'Tradition,'" *Critical Review of International Social and Political Philosophy* 20, no. 3 (2017): 296–313, https://doi.org/10.1080/13698230.2017.1293914. See, most importantly, Girard, *The Scapegoat*; Girard, *Violence and the Sacred*; René Girard, *I See Satan Fall Like Lightning*, trans. James G. Williams (Maryknoll, NY: Orbis Books, 2001); René Girard and Benoît Chantre, *Battling to the End: Conversations with Benoît Chantre* (East Lansing: Michigan State University Press, 2010).

21. Hedley Bull, "International Theory: The Case for a Classical Approach," *World Politics* 18, no. 3 (1966): 361–77.

22. Martin Hollis and Steve Smith, *Explaining and Understanding International Relations* (New York: Oxford University Press, 1990).

23. Mervyn Frost and Silviya Lechner, "Understanding International Practices from the Internal Point of View," *Journal of International Political Theory* 12, no. 3 (2016): 313, https://doi.org/10.1177/1755088215596765.

24. Christer Jönsson and Martin Hall, *Essence of Diplomacy* (London: Palgrave Macmillan, 2005), 14. See also Patrick T. Jackson and D. H. Nexon, "Relations Before States: Substance, Process and the Study of World Politics," *European Journal of International Relations* 5, no. 3 (1999): 291–332.

25. Jenny Edkins and Maja Zehfuss, "Generalising the International," *Review of International Studies* 31, no. 3 (2005): 471. See also Hedley Bull, *The Anarchical*

Society: A Study of Order in World Politics, 4th ed. (London: Palgrave Macmillan, 2012).

26. Michael Howard, *The Invention of Peace: Reflections on War and International Order* (New Haven, CT: Yale University Press, 2001).

27. Brighi and Cerella, "An Alternative Vision of Politics and Violence," 18–19.

28. Hans J. Morgenthau, Hartmut Behr, and Felix Rösch, *The Concept of the Political* (London: Palgrave Macmillan, 2012).

29. Friedrich Kratochwil, *Praxis: On Acting and Knowing* (Cambridge: Cambridge University Press, 2018), 1.

30. Fareed Zakaria, *The Post-American World: Release 2.0* (New York: W. W. Norton, 2011), 35. See also Francis Fukuyama, *Political Order and Political Decay: From the Industrial Revolution to the Globalization of Democracy* (London: Farrar Straus and Giroux, 2014), 186–87; John J. Mearsheimer, *The Great Delusion: Liberal Dreams and International Realities* (New Haven, CT: Yale University Press, 2018).

31. Paul Laurent and Gilles Paquet, "Intercultural Relations: A Myrdal—Tocqueville—Girard Interpretative Scheme," *International Political Science Review* 12, no. 3 (1991): 171–83; René Girard and Henri Tincq, "What Is Happening Today Is Mimetic Rivalry on a Global Scale," *South Central Revue* 19, nos. 2/3 (2002): 22–27. On the critical, some might argue conservative notion of Realism, see L. Finlayson, "With Radicals Like These, Who Needs Conservatives? Doom, Gloom, and Realism in Political Theory," *European Journal of Political Theory* 16, no. 3 (2017): 264–82; Felix Rösch, "Realism as Social Criticism: The Thinking Partnership of Hannah Arendt and Hans Morgenthau," *International Politics* 50, no. 6 (2013): 815–29.

32. Girard, *Violence and the Sacred*, 49.

33. See also Jonathan C. Agensky, "Recognizing Religion: Politics, History, and the 'Long 19th Century,'" *European Journal of International Relations* 23 (2017): 729–55, https://doi.org/10.1177/1354066116681428; Mona Kanwal Sheikh, "How Does Religion Matter? Pathways to Religion in International Relations," *Review of International Studies* 38 (2012): 492–507, https://doi.org/10.1017/S026021051100057X; Samantha May, Erin K. Wilson, Claudia Baumgart-Ochse, and Faiz Sheikh, "The Religious as Political and the Political as Religious: Globalisation, Post-Secularism and the Shifting Boundaries of the Sacred," *Politics, Religion & Ideology* 15, no. 3 (2014): 331–46; Michael Walzer, *Thinking Politically: Essays in Political Theory* (New Haven, CT: Yale University Press, 2007), 147–67.

34. See, for example, Thomas, "Culture, Religion and Violence."

35. Scott M. Thomas, *The Global Resurgence of Religion and the Transformation of International Relations: The Struggle for the Soul of the Twenty-First Century* (London: Palgrave Macmillan, 2005). Elizabeth Shakman Hurd, *The Politics of Secularism in International Relations* (Princeton, NJ: Princeton University Press, 2008).

36. John Wooldridge and Adrian Micklethwait, *God Is Back: How the Global Revival*

of Faith Is Challenging the World (London: Penguin Books, 2009). See also Jack
L. Snyder, ed., *Religion and International Relations Theory* (New York: Columbia
University Press, 2011); Monica Duffy Toft, Daniel Philpott, and Timothy Samuel
Shah, *God's Century: Resurgent Religion and Global Politics* (New York: W. W. Norton,
2011). Nukhet A. Sandal and Patrick James, "Religion and International Relations
Theory: Towards a Mutual Understanding," *European Journal of International Relations*
17, no. 1 (2011): 3–25.

37. See, for example, Agensky, "Recognizing Religion."

38. Nicolas Guilhot, "American Katechon: When Political Theology Became International
Relations Theory," *Constellations* 17, no. 2 (2010): 224–53.

39. See, for example, Antonio Cerella, "Until the End of the World: Girard, Schmitt and
the Origins of Violence," *Journal of International Political Theory* 11, no. 1 (2015):
42–60, https://doi.org/10.1177/1755088214555457; Girard, *Violence and the Sacred*;
René Girard, "On War and Apocalypse," *First Things*, August/September 2009; Girard
and Chantre, *Battling to the End*; René Girard and Wolfgang Palaver, *Gewalt Und
Religion, Ursache Oder Wirkung?* (Berlin: Matthes & Seitz, 2010); Robert Hamerton-
Kelly, ed., *Violent Origins: Walter Burkert, René Girard & Jonathan Z. Smith on Ritual
Killing and Cultural Formation* (Stanford, CA: Stanford University Press, 1987);
Scott Cowdell, Chris Fleming, and Joel Hodge, eds., *Violence, Desire, and the Sacred:
Girard's Mimetic Theory Across the Disciplines* (New York: Continuum, 2012); Scott
Cowdell, Chris Fleming, and Joel Hodge, eds., *Violence, Desire, and the Sacred*, vol. 2,
René Girard and Sacrifice in Life, Love, and Literature (London: Bloomsbury, 2014);
Scott M. Thomas, "Rethinking Religious Violence: Towards a Mimetic Approach to
Violence in International Relations," *Journal of International Political Theory* 11, no. 1
(2015): 61–79; Roberto Farneti, "Bipolarity Redux: The Mimetic Context of the 'New
Wars,'" *Cambridge Review of International Affairs* 26, no. 1 (2013): 181–202, https://
doi.org/10.1080/09557571.2012.737305; Farneti, *Mimetic Politics*.

40. See for example Roberto Farneti, "A Mimetic Perspective on Conflict Resolution,"
Polity 41, no. 4 (2009): 536–58, https://doi.org/10.1057/pol.2009.2; Andrew
Marr, *Tools for Peace: The Spiritual Craft of St. Benedict and René Girard* (New York:
iUniverse, 2007); Vern Neufled Redekop and Thomas Ryba, eds., *René Girard and
Creative Reconciliation* (Lanham, MD: Lexington Books, 2014).

41. Girard, *I See Satan Fall like Lightning*, 15.

42. Robert Jervis, *Perception and Misperception in International Politics* (Princeton, NJ:
Princeton University Press, 1976); Graham T. Allison, *Essence of Decision: Explaining
the Cuban Missile Crisis*, 2nd ed. (Boston: Little, Brown, 1971).

43. Hans J. Morgenthau, *Scientific Man vs. Power Politics* (Chicago: University of Chicago
Press, 1946), 195.

44. Clifford Geertz, *Local Knowledge: Further Essays in Interpretative Anthropology* (New
York: Basic Books, 1983), 143. Like Geertz, Ernst Kantorowitcz points out the relation
of religious ideas and symbols to the secular world and the question of what constitutes

modernity. Ernst Kantorowicz, *The King's Two Bodies: A Study in Mediaeval Political Theology*, 7th ed. (Princeton, NJ: Princeton University Press, 1997).

45. Richard Ned Lebow, *The Tragic Vision of Politics: Ethics, Interests and Orders* (Cambridge: Cambridge University Press, 2003); Alister Wedderburn, "Tragedy, Genealogy and Theories of International Relations," *European Journal of International Relations* 3, no. 2 (2017): https://doi.org/10.1177/1354066116689131.

46. Vassilios Paipais, "Between Politics and the Political: Reading Hans J. Morgenthau's Double Critique of Depoliticiastion," *Millennium: Journal of International Studies* 42, no. 2 (2014): 369.

47. Jönsson and Hall, *Essence of Diplomacy*, 14.

CHAPTER 1. INTERNATIONAL POLITICS AND REALIST THOUGHT

1. On Realism see, for example, Nicolas Guilhot, *After the Enlightenment: Political Realism and International Relations in the Mid-Twentieth Century* (Cambridge: Cambridge University Press, 2017). Kenneth Waltz aptly captured the epistemological difference between classical Realism and Neorealism in the title of one of his articles: "Realist Thought and Neorealist Theory," *Journal of International Affairs* 44, no. 1 (1990): 21–37. I do not equate Realism with the "unrealism" of contemporary neo-Realism or neo-classical Realism. See, in particular, Ido Oren, "The Unrealism of Contemporary Realism: The Tension Between Realist Theory and Realists' Practice," *Perspectives on Politics* 7, no. 2 (2009): 283–301. For a recent comprehensive literature review on the topic see Duncan Bell, "Political Realism and International Relations," *Philosophy Compass* 12, no. 2 (2017), https://doi.org/10.1111/phc3.12403. The English School also transformed into a positivist research enterprise. At worst, this bullies the three traditions of Martin Wight into a three-folded typology of international politics. At best, this keeps open the possibilities the English School offers to take into consideration relational elements of international political conduct. Martin Wight, *International Theory: The Three Traditions* (Leicester: Leicester University Press, 1991).

2. Elisabetta Brighi and Antonio Cerella, "An Alternative Vision of Politics and Violence: Introducing Mimetic Theory in International Studies," *Journal of International Political Theory* 11, no. 1 (2015): 17–18.

3. Alison McQueen, "Political Realism and Moral Corruption," *European Journal of Political Theory* (2016): 1–2.

4. Daniel M. Green, "Introduction to the English School in International Studies," in *Guide to the English School in International Studies*, ed. Cornelia Navari and Daniel M. Green (West Sussex: Wiley-Blackwell, 2014), 1.

5. Marysia Zalewski, "'All These Theories yet the Bodies Keep Piling up': Theory, Theorists, Theorising," in *Positivism and Beyond*, ed. Steve Smith, Ken Booth, and Marysia Zalewski (Cambridge: Cambridge University Press, 1996), 340–53. Robert

W. Cox, "Social Forces, States and World Orders: Beyond International Relations Theory," *Millennium: Journal of International Studies* 10, no. 2 (1981): 126–55, https://doi.org/10.1177/03058298810100020501.

6. Ryan P. Hanley, "Political Science and Political Understanding: Isaiah Berlin on the Nature of Political Inquiry," *American Political Science Review* 98, no. 2 (2004): 338, https://doi.org/10.1017/S0003055404001170.

7. Scott M. Thomas, *The Global Resurgence of Religion and the Transformation of International Relations: The Struggle for the Soul of the Twenty-First Century* (New York: Palgrave Macmillan, 2005), 73.

8. Thomas Nagel, *The View from Nowhere* (Oxford: Oxford University Press, 1989).

9. Mark Bevir and R. A. W. Rhodes, "Interpretive Theory," in *Theory and Methods in Political Science*, ed. David Marsh and Gerry Stoker, 2nd ed. (London: Palgrave Macmillan, 2002), 132, 133; Cecelia Lynch, *Interpreting International Politics* (New York: Routledge, 2014); Peregrine Schwartz-Shea and Dvora Yanow, *Interpretive Research Design: Concepts and Processes* (New York: Routledge, 2012).

10. Robert A. Isaak, *Individuals and World Politics* (North Scituate, MA: Duxbury Press, 1975), 256.

11. Robert Jackson, *The Global Covenant: Human Conduct in a World of States* (New York: Oxford University Press, 2000).

12. Quoted in Christer Jönsson and Martin Hall, *Essence of Diplomacy* (London: Palgrave Macmillan, 2005), 14. See also Patrick T. Jackson and D. H. Nexon, "Relations Before States: Substance, Process and the Study of World Politics," *European Journal of International Relations* 5, no. 3 (1999): 291–332.

13. William Bain, *Between Anarchy and Society: Trusteeship and the Obligations of Power* (Oxford: Oxford University Press, 2004), 9.

14. Martha Finnemore, *National Interests in International Society* (Ithaca, NY: Cornell University Press, 1996).

15. Michael C. Williams, "Why Ideas Matter in International Relations: Hans Morgenthau, Classical Realism, and the Moral Construction of Power Politics," *International Organization* 58, no. 4 (2004): 633–65, https://doi.org/10.1017/S0020818304040202. See, most prominently, Judith Goldstein and Robert O. Keohane, eds., *Ideas and Foreign Policy: Beliefs, Institutions, and Political Change* (Ithaca, NY: Cornell University Press, 1993).

16. Alasdair MacIntyre, *After Virtue: A Study in Moral Theory* (Notre Dame, IN: University of Notre Dame Press, 1981). See also Jodok Troy, *Christian Approaches to International Affairs* (London: Palgrave Macmillan, 2012), chap. 4. Thomas, *The Global Resurgence*, 90

17. Thomas, *The Global Resurgence*, 90. See also Jeroen Gunning and Richard Jackson, "What's So 'Religious' about 'Religious Terrorism'?," *Critical Studies on Terrorism* 4 (2011): 369–88, https://doi.org/10.1080/17539153.2011.623405; Anna

Grzymala-Busse, "The Difficulty with Doctrine: How Religion Can Influence Politics,"
Government and Opposition 51 (2016): 327–50, https://doi.org/10.1017/gov.2015.38.

18. Charles Tilly, *Collective Violence* (Cambridge: Cambridge University Press, 2003),
6. On this aspect of theorizing international politics in the context of recent trends
in International Relation's theory, see David M. McCourt, "Practice Theory and
Relationalism as the New Constructivism," *International Studies Quarterly* 60, no. 3
(2016): 475–85.

19. Hedley Bull, "International Theory: The Case for a Classical Approach," *World Politics*
18, no. 3 (1966); William Bain, "Deconfusing Morgenthau: Moral Inquiry and
Classical Realism Reconsidered," *Review of International Studies* 26, no. 3 (2000).

20. Ido Oren, *Our Enemies and US: America's Rivalries and the Making of Political Science*
(Ithaca, NY: Cornell University Press, 2003); Patrick Thaddeus Jackson, *The Conduct of
Inquiry in International Relations* (London: Routledge, 2009).

21. Hans J. Morgenthau, *Politics Among Nations: The Struggle for Power and Peace* (New
York: Knopf, 1948), 7.

22. Cornelia Navari, "Introduction: Methods and Methodology in the English School," in
Theorising International Society: English School Methods, ed. Cornelia Navari (London:
Palgrave Macmillan, 2009), 3.

23. Martin Wight, "Western Values in International Relations," in *Diplomatic
Investigations: Essays in the Theory of International Politics*, ed. Herbert Butterfield and
Martin Wight (London: Allen & Unwin, 1966), 130.

24. Jönsson and Hall, *Essence of Diplomacy*, 25.

25. Navari, "Introduction," 5.

26. See also Seán Molloy, "Truth, Power, Theory: Hans Morgenthau's Formulation
of Realism," *Diplomacy & Statecraft* 15, no. 1 (2004): 1–34, https://doi.
org/10.1080/09592290490438042.

27. Chris Brown, "The 'Practice Turn,' Phronesis and Classical Realism: Towards a
Phronetic International Political Theory?," *Millennium: Journal of International Studies*
40, no. 3 (2012): 440.

28. Cornelia Navari, "The Concept of Practice in the English School," *European Journal
of International Relations* 17, no. 4 (2011): 611–30. Navari, "Introduction," 18. See
also Frost and Lechner's equally (as to the English School) critical assessment of the
epistemology and ontology of recent studies on international practices. Mervyn
Frost and Silviya Lechner, "Understanding International Practices from the Internal
Point of View," *Journal of International Political Theory* 12, no. 3 (2016): 299–319,
https://doi.org/10.1177/1755088215596765; Mervyn Frost and Silviya Lechner,
"Two Conceptions of International Practice: Aristotelian Praxis or Wittgensteinian
Language-Games?," *Review of International Studies* 42, no. 2 (2016): 334–50, https://
doi.org/10.1017/S0260210515000169.

29. See, for example, Marc Trachtenberg, *The Craft of International History: A Guide to Method* (Princeton, NJ: Princeton University Press, 2006).

30. Navari, "The Concept of Practice in the English School," 614.

31. Wight, "Western Values in International Relations," 116.

32. Navari, "The Concept of Practice in the English School," 620.

33. Navari, "The Concept of Practice in the English School," 621.

34. Jackson, *The Global Covenant*, 78.

35. MacIntyre, *After Virtue*, 175. See also Michael Oakeshott, *On Human Conduct* (Oxford: Clarendon Press, 1975).

36. Cornelia Navari, "English School Methodology," in Navari and Green, *Guide to the English School in International Studies*, 213. See also Hans J. Morgenthau, *Politics Among Nations: The Struggle for Power and Peace*, 5th ed. (New York: A. A. Knopf, 1973), 5.

37. Barry Buzan, *From International to World Society? English School Theory and the Social Structure of Globalisation* (Cambridge: Cambridge University Press, 2004); Finnemore, *National Interests in International Society*, 17–19.

38. See, for example, Alison McQueen, "The Case for Kinship: Classical Realism and Political Realism," in *Politics Recovered: Realist Thought in Theory and Practice*, ed. Matt Sleat (New York: Columbia University Press, 2018); Nicolas Guilhot, ed., *The Invention of International Relations Theory: Realism, the Rockefeller Foundation, and the 1954 Conference on Theory* (New York: Columbia University Press, 2011); Joseph M. Parent and Joshua M. Baron, "Elder Abuse: How the Moderns Mistreat Classical Realism," *International Studies Review* 13 (2011): 193–213; Richard K. Ashley, "Political Realism and Human Interest," *International Studies Quarterly* 25 (1981): 204–36; Bain, "Deconfusing Morgenthau"; J. S. Barkin, "Constructivism, Realism, and the Variety of Human Natures," in *Human Beings in International Relations*, ed. Daniel Jacobi and Annette Freyberg-Inan (Cambridge: Cambridge University Press, 2015), 156–71; Hartmut Behr and Amelia Heath, "Misreading in IR Theory and Ideology Critique: Morgenthau, Waltz and Neo-Realism," *Review of International Studies* 35 (2009): 327–49; Murielle Cozette, "Realistic Realism? American Political Realism, Clausewitz and Raymond Aron on the Problem of Means and Ends in International Politics," *Journal of Strategic Studies* 27, no. 3 (2004): 428–53; Murielle Cozette, "What Lies Ahead: Classical Realism on the Future of International Relations," *International Studies Review* 10 (2008): 667–79; Campbell Craig, *Glimmer of a New Leviathan: Total War in the Realism of Niebuhr, Morgenthau, and Waltz* (New York: Columbia University Press, 2007); Oren, "The Unrealism of Contemporary Realism"; Vassilios Paipais, "Necessary Fiction: Realism's Tragic Theology," *International Politics* 50, no. 6 (2013), https://doi.org/10.1057/ip.2013.38; William E. Scheuerman, *Hans Morgenthau: Realism and Beyond* (Cambridge, UK: Polity Press, 2009); Ronald H. Stone, *Prophetic Realism: Beyond Militarism and Pacifism in an Age of Terror* (New York: T & T Clark, 2005); Michael C. Williams, ed., *Realism Reconsidered: The Legacy*

of Hans Morgenthau in International Relations (Oxford: Oxford University Press, 2007).

39. Hans J. Morgenthau, Hartmut Behr, and Felix Rösch, *The Concept of the Political* (London: Palgrave Macmillan, 2012), 47.

40. Hannah Arendt, *The Human Condition*, 2nd ed. (Chicago: University of Chicago Press, 2006).

41. Hans J. Morgenthau, "An Intellectual Autobiography," *Society in Transition* 15 (1978): 67. See also Robert Schuett, "Freudian Roots of Political Realism: Importance of Sigmund Freud to Hans J. Morgenthau's Theory of International Power Politics," *History of the Human Sciences* 20, no. 4 (2007): 53–78; Robert Schuett, *Political Realism, Freud, and Human Nature in International Relations: The Resurrection of the Realist Man* (New York: Palgrave Macmillan, 2009); Robert Schuett, "Classical Realism, Freud and Human Nature in International Relations," *History of the Human Sciences* 23, no. 2 (2010): 21–46.

42. Hans J. Morgenthau, *Politics Among Nations: The Struggle for Power and Peace*, 5th ed. (New York: Alfred A. Knopf, 1973), pt. 2.

43. Martti Koskenniemi, *The Gentle Civilizer of Nations: The Rise and Fall of International Law, 1870–1960* (Cambridge: Cambridge University Press, 2002), 454.

44. S. Turner and G. Mazur, "Morgenthau as a Weberian Methodologist," *European Journal of International Relations* 15, no. 3 (2009): 477–504, https://doi.org/10.1177/1354066109338242. See also Oren, "The Unrealism of Contemporary Realism"; Bain, "Deconfusing Morgenthau."

45. Oren, "The Unrealism of Contemporary Realism"; Turner and Mazur, "Morgenthau as a Weberian Methodologist."

46. Clifford Geertz, "Thick Description: Toward an Interpretative Theory of Culture," in *The Interpretation of Cultures*, ed. Clifford Geertz (New York: Basic Books, 1973), 5–6.

47. Jörg Friedrichs and Friedrich Kratochwil, "On Acting and Knowing: How Pragmatism Can Advance International Relations Research and Methodology," *International Organization* 63, no. 4 (2009): 714–15, https://doi.org/10.1017/S0020818309990142.

48. Schwartz-Shea and Yanow, *Interpretive Research Design*, 27.

49. James N. Rosenau, "Probing Puzzles Persistently: A Desirable but Improbable Future for IR Theory," in Smith, Booth, and Zalewski, *Positivism and Beyond*; Cox, "Social Forces, States and World Orders."

50. Ole J. Sending, Vincent Pouliot, and Iver B. Neumann, "Introduction," in *Diplomacy and the Making of World Politics*, ed. Ole J. Sending, Vincent Pouliot, and Iver B. Neumann (Cambridge: Cambridge University Press, 2015), 9.

CHAPTER 2. DESIRE FOR POWER AND THE POWER OF DESIRE

1. See, for example, Chris Brown, "International Relations and International Political Theory," in *The Oxford Handbook of International Political Theory*, ed. Chris Brown and Robyn Eckersley (Oxford: Oxford University Press, 2018), 48–59.

2. Wolfgang Palaver, *René Girard's Mimetic Theory* (East Lansing: Michigan State University Press, 2013), 168–71; Ysabel Johnston, "Mimesis and Ritual: Girardian Critique of the Social Contract," *Res Cogitans* 5, no. 1 (2014): 169–77.

3. The possible exception is one of Girard's first major works (which originally appeared in 1965) and a newly revised edition of it. René Girard, *Deceit, Desire, and the Novel: Self and Other in Literary Structure* (Baltimore: Johns Hopkins University Press, 1976); René Girard, *Das Ende der Gewalt: Analyse des Menschheitsverhängnisses* (Freiburg im Breisgau: Herder, 1983).

4. If Morgenthau can be called a Realist at all. This book argues that Morgenthau is not the "Realist" as textbooks characterize him. William E. Scheuerman, "Was Morgenthau a Realist? Revisiting Scientific Man vs. Power Politics," *Constellations* 14, no. 4 (2007): 506–30.

5. Hans J. Morgenthau, "Positivism, Functionalism, and International Law," *American Journal of International Law* 34, no. 2 (1940): 284.

6. See, in particular, the contributions to the special issue in *International Political Theory* 11, no. 1 (2015); Roberto Farneti, "A Mimetic Perspective on Conflict Resolution," *Polity* 41, no. 4 (2009): 536–58, https://doi.org/10.1057/pol.2009.2; Roberto Farneti, "Bipolarity Redux: The Mimetic Context of the 'New Wars,'" *Cambridge Review of International Affairs* 26, no. 1 (2013): 181–202, https://doi.org/10.1080/09557571.2 012.737305; Richard Sakwa, "The Cold Peace: Russo-Western Relations as a Mimetic Cold War," *Cambridge Review of International Affairs* 26, no. 1 (2013): 203–24, https://doi.org/10.1080/09557571.2012.710584. Others, such as Franeti's *Mimetic Politics: Dyadic Patterns in Global Politics* (East Lansing: Michigan State University Press, 2015), focus on political theory.

7. See, for example, Necati Polat, *International Relations, Meaning and Mimesis* (New York: Routledge, 2012); Scott M. Thomas, *The Global Resurgence of Religion and the Transformation of International Relations: The Struggle for the Soul of the Twenty-First Century* (New York: Palgrave Macmillan, 2005). Thomas's and others' turn to mimetic theory in order to approach International Relations problems are now more commonly picked up by International Relations studies. Thomas, *The Global Resurgence*, particularly chap. 5; Scott M. Thomas, "Culture, Religion and Violence: Rene Girard's Mimetic Theory," *Millennium: Journal of International Studies* 43, no. 1 (2014): 308–27. See particularly issue 1, vol. 11 (2015) of the *Journal of International Political Theory*. Elisabetta Brighi and Antonio Cerella, "An Alternative Vision of Politics and Violence: Introducing Mimetic Theory in International Studies," *Journal of International Political Theory* 11, no. 1 (2015): 3–25.

8. For the following summary of Girard's thoughts, particularly regarding competition

and enmity, see Wolfgang Palaver, "René Girard's Contribution to Political Theology: Overcoming Deadlocks of Competition and Enmity," in *Between Philosophy and Theology: Contemporary Interpretations of Christianity*, ed. L. Boeve and Christophe Brabant (Burlington, VT: Ashgate Pub., 2010), 149–65.

9. Rowan Williams, "Foreword," in *Can We Survive Our Origins? Readings in René Girard's Theory of Violence and the Sacred*, ed. Pierpaolo Antonello and Paul Gifford (East Lansing: Michigan State University Press, 2015), xii.

10. Plato, *The Republic*, ed. G. R. F. Ferraris, trans. T. Griffith (Cambridge: Cambridge University Press, 2000), 205; Augustine, *Concerning the City of God Against the Pagans*, trans. H. Bettension (London: Penguin Books, 2003), 324.

11. Palaver, "René Girard's Contribution to Political Theology," 159. The biblical Decalogue especially addresses this problem by stating that "You shall not covet your neighbor's house, you shall not covet your neighbor's wife, or male or female slave, or ox, of donkey, or anything that belongs to your neighbor." Exod. 20:17.

12. Girard, *Das Ende der Gewalt*, 204.

13. René Girard, *Evolution and Conversation: Dialogues on the Origin of Culture*, with Pierpaolo Antonello and Joao Cezar de Castro Rocha (London: Continuum, 2008), 59–60.

14. René Girard, "Triangular Desire," in *The Girard Reader*, ed. René Girard and James G. Williams (New York: Crossroad and Herder, 1996), 33–44.

15. Thomas, *The Global Resurgence*, 124.

16. Sigmund Freud, James Strachey and Albert Dickson, *Civilization, Society and Religion: Group Psychology, Civilization and Its Discontents and Other Works* (London: Penguin Books, 1991); Anton Blok, "The Narcissism of Minor Differences," *European Journal of Social Theory* 1, no. 1 (1998): 33–56.

17. Pierre Bourdieu, *Distinction: A Social Critique of the Judgement of Taste*, trans. Richard Nice (London: Routledge, 1984), 479.

18. Vern Neufled Redekop and Thomas Ryba, "Introduction: Deep-Rooted Conflict, Reconsiliation, and Mimetic Theory," in *René Girard and Creative Reconciliation*, ed. Vern Neufled Redekop and Thomas Ryba (Lanham, MD: Lexington Books, 2014), 4; René Girard and Benoît Chantre, *Im Angesicht der Apokalypse: Clausewitz zu Ende Denken; Gespräche mit Benoît Chantre* (Berlin: Matthes et Seitz Berlin, 2014), 83.

19. Hans Magnus Enzensberger, *Civil War* (London: Granta Books, 1994). See also J. Beall, T. Goodfellow, and D. Rodgers, "Cities and Conflict in Fragile States in the Developing World," *Urban Studies* 50, no. 15 (2013): 1–19, https://doi.org/10.1177/0042098013487775.

20. Victor E. Frankl, *Man's Search for Meaning* (London: Rider, 2004), 153–54.

21. René Girard, *Ich sah den Satan vom Himmel fallen wie einen Blitz: Eine kritische Apologie Des Christentums* (Munich: Hanser, 2002), 23.

22. See, for example, Francis Fukuyama, *Political Order and Political Decay: From the Industrial Revolution to the Globalization of Democracy* (London: Farrar Straus and Giroux, 2014), 186–87.

23. René Girard, *The One by Whom Scandal Comes* (East Lansing: Michigan State University Press, 2014), 4–5.

24. See also Paul Laurent and Gilles Paquet, "Intercultural Relations: A Myrdal—Tocqueville—Girard Interpretative Scheme," *International Political Science Review* 12, no. 3 (1991): 171–83.

25. René Girard, *A Theater of Envy: William Shakespeare* (Oxford: Oxford University Press, 1991), 186; René Girard, *Things Hidden Since the Foundation of the World: Research Undertaken in Collaboration with Jean-Michel Oughourlian and Guy Lefort*, trans. Michael Metteer (book 1) and Stephen Bann (books 2 & 3) (London: Athlone Press, 1987), 26.

26. Palaver, "René Girard's Contribution to Political Theology," 153. For a critical view on this aspect in the context of the origins of religion see, for example, Richard Stivers, "The Festival in Light of the Theory of the Three Milieus: A Critique of Girard's Theory of Ritual Scapegoating," *Journal of the American Academy of Religion* 61, no. 3 (1993): 505–38.

27. René Girard and Henri Tincq, "What Is Happening Today Is Mimetic Rivalry on a Global Scale," *South Central Revue* 19, nos. 2/3 (2002): 22–27; René Girard and Benoît Chantre, *Battling to the End: Conversations with Benoît Chantre* (East Lansing: Michigan State University Press, 2010); René Girard, "On War and Apocalypse," *First Things*, August/September 2009; Girard and Chantre, *Im Angesicht der Apokalypse*; Curtis Gruenler, "C. S. Lewis and René Girard on Desire, Conversion, and Myth: The Case of 'till We Have Faces,'" *Christianity & Literature* 60, no. 2 (2011): 247–65; Wilhelm Guggenberger and Wolfgang Palaver, eds., *Eskalation zum Aussersten? Girards Clausewitz interdisziplinar kommentiert* (Baden-Baden: Nomos Verlagsgesellschaft, 2015).

28. René Girard, *Figuren des Begehrens: Das Selbst und der Andere in der fiktionalen Realität* (Wien: LIT, 1999); Girard, *Deceit, Desire, and the Novel*. René Girard, *The Scapegoat* (Baltimore: Johns Hopkins University Press, 1986).

29. René Girard, *Violence and the Sacred* (Baltimore: Johns Hopkins University Press, 1979). See also Paul W. Kahn, *Sacred Violence: Torture, Terror, and Sovereignty* (Ann Arbor: University of Michigan Press, 2008).

30. Girard, *Violence and the Sacred*.

31. Scott R. Appleby, *The Ambivalence of the Sacred: Religion, Violence, and Reconciliation* (Lanham, MD: Rowman & Littlefield, 2000).

32. See, for example, Vern Neufled Redekop and Thomas Ryba, eds., *René Girard and Creative Reconciliation* (Lanham, MD: Lexington Books, 2014); Cecelia Lynch, "A Neo-Weberian Approach to Religion in International Politics," *International Theory* 1,

no. 3 (2009): 381–408; Anna Grzymala-Busse, "The Difficulty with Doctrine: How Religion Can Influence Politics," *Government and Opposition* 51 (2016): 327–50, https://doi.org/10.1017/gov.2015.38.

33. Gregorio Bettiza and Filippo Dionigi, "How Do Religious Norms Diffuse? Institutional Translation and International Change in a Post-Secular World Society," *European Journal of International Relations* 21, no. 3 (2015): 621–46.

34. Austin Dacey, *The Secular Conscience: Why Belief Belongs in Public Life* (Amherst, NY: Prometheus Books, 2008); Jürgen Habermas, *Glauben und Wissen* (Frankfurt: Suhrkamp, 2001), 24.

35. Stephen L. Gardner, "Rene Girard's Apocalyptic Critique of Historical Reason: Limiting Politics to Make Way for Faith," *Contagion: Journal of Violence, Mimesis, and Culture* 18 (2011): 1–22.

36. Girard and Chantre, *Battling to the End*.

37. Mark Juergensmeyer, *The New Cold War? Religious Nationalism Confronts the Secular State* (Berkeley: University of California Press, 1994); Mark Juergensmeyer, *Global Rebellion: Religious Challenges to the Secular State from Christian Militias to Al Qaeda* (Berkeley: University of California Press, 2008); Sabina Mihelj, "'Faith in Nation Comes in Different Guises': Modernist Versions of Religious Nationalism," *Nations and Nationalism* 13, no. 2 (2007): 265–84.

38. Max Weber, *Wirtschaft und Gesellschaft : Grundriss der verstehenden Soziologie*, vol. 5, ed. von Johannes Winckelmann (Tübingen: J.C.B. Mohr (Paul Siebeck), 1980), I, §17. Hans J. Morgenthau, "The Evil of Politics and the Ethics of Evil," *Ethics* 56, no. 1 (1945): 1–18.

39. Morgenthau, "The Evil of Politics and the Ethics of Evil."

40. Émile Durkheim, *The Elementary Forms of the Religious Life*, trans. Joseph Ward Swain (Mineola, NY: Dover Publications Inc., 2008); Mircea Eliade, *The Sacred and the Profane: The Nature of Religion*, trans. Willard R. Trask (San Diego: Harcourt, 1987).

41. Hans J. Morgenthau, "The Twilight of International Morality," *Ethics* 58, no. 2 (1948): 99.

42. Girard, *The Scapegoat*; Girard, *Violence and the Sacred*; Robert Hamerton-Kelly, ed., *Violent Origins: Walter Burkert, René Girard & Jonathan Z. Smith on Ritual Killing and Cultural Formation* (Stanford: Stanford University Press, 1987). For a concise introduction to this issue, particularly in the context of Christianity, see Giles Fraser, *Christianity and Violence: Girard, Nietzsche, Anselm and Tutu* (London: Darton, Longman and Todd, 2001).

43. Palaver, "René Girard's Contribution to Political Theology," 159; Wolfgang Palaver, "Envy or Emulation: A Christian Understanding of Economic Passions," in *Passions in Economy, Politics, and the Media: In Discussion with Christian Theology*, ed. Wolfgang Palaver and Petra Steinmair-Pösel (Münster: LIT, 2005), 150–51.

44. René Girard, *Das Heilige und die Gewalt* (Düsseldorf: Patmos, 2006), 381.

45. It is thus that Pope John Paul II emphasized the importance of spiritual goods to build peace. "It is easy to see that material goods do not have unlimited capacity for satisfying the needs of man: They are not in themselves easily distributed and, in the relationship between those who possess and enjoy them and those who are without them, they give rise to tension, dissension and division that will often even turn into open conflict. Spiritual goods, on the other hand, are open to unlimited enjoyment by many at the same time, without diminution of the goods themselves. Indeed, the more people share in such goods, the more they are enjoyed and drawn upon, the more then do those goods show their indestructible and immortal worth. This truth is confirmed, for example, by the works of creativity—I mean by the works of thought, poetry, music, and the figurative arts, fruits of man's spirit." John Paul II, "Address to the United Nations General Assembly," New Advent, http://www.newadvent.org/library/docs_jp02u1.htm.

46. Morgenthau, "The Evil of Politics and the Ethics of Evil."

47. Mona K. Sheikh, "Appointing Evil in International Relations," *International Politics* 51, no. 4 (2014): 499; Hans J. Morgenthau, *Scientific Man vs. Power Politics* (Chicago: University of Chicago Press, 1946), 203.

48. Robert A. Isaak, *Individuals and World Politics* (North Scituate, MA: Duxbury Press, 1975), 5.

49. Isaak, *Individuals and World Politics*, 256.

50. Hans J. Morgenthau, Hartmut Behr, and Felix Rösch, *The Concept of the Political* (London: Palgrave Macmillan, 2012).

51. Jeffrey W. Taliaferro, Steven E. Lobell, and Norrin M. Ripsman, "Introduction: Neoclassical Realism, the State, and Foreign Policy," in *Neoclassical Realism, the State, and Foreign Policy*, ed. Steven E. Lobell, Norrin M. Ripsman, and Jeffrey W. Taliaferro (Cambridge: Cambridge University Press, 2009), 14–15; Ken Booth and Nicholas J. Wheeler, *The Security Dilemma: Fear, Cooperation, and Trust in World Politics* (London: Palgrave Macmillan, 2008).

52. Morgenthau, "Positivism, Functionalism, and International Law," 284.

53. Alexander Wendt, *Social Theory of International Politics* (Cambridge: Cambridge University Press, 1999), 131.

54. See the critical discussion of the literature on this point in William E. Scheuerman, "The Realist Revival in Political Philosophy, or: Why New Is Not Always Improved," *International Politics* 50, no. 6 (2013): 798–814.

55. J. Samuel Barkin, *Realist Constructivism: Rethinking International Relations Theory* (Cambridge: Cambridge University Press, 2010), 18–20.

56. Doing so, Realism follows Republicans (e.g., Hanna Arendt), conservatives (e.g., Michael Oakeshott), and liberals alike (e.g., Isaiah Berlin).

57. Vassilios Paipais, "Between Politics and the Political: Reading Hans J. Morgenthau's

Double Critique of Depoliticiastion," *Millennium: Journal of International Studies* 42, no. 2 (2014): 369.

58. Morgenthau, "The Evil of Politics and the Ethics of Evil," 11.

59. Benjamin Herborth, "Imagining Man—Forgetting Society?," in *Human Beings in International Relations*, ed. Daniel Jacobi and Annette Freyberg-Inan (Cambridge: Cambridge University Press, 2015), 233. See also Richard Ned Lebow, *The Tragic Vision of Politics: Ethics, Interests and Orders* (Cambridge: Cambridge University Press, 2003); Vassilios Paipais, "Necessary Fiction: Realism's Tragic Theology," *International Politics* 50, no. 6 (2013): 354–75, https://doi.org/10.1057/ip.2013.38; Mark Chou, "Morgenthau, the Tragic: On Tragedy and the Transition from Scientific Man to Politics Among Nations," *Telos*, no. 157 (2011): 109–28, https://doi.org/10.3817/1211157109; Alister Wedderburn, "Tragedy, Genealogy and Theories of International Relations," *European Journal of International Relations* 3, no. 2 (2017), https://doi.org/10.1177/1354066116689131; Felix Rösch, "Pouvoir, Puissance, and Politics: Hans Morgenthau's Dualistic Concept of Power?," *Review of International Studies* 40 (2014): 353–54, https://doi.org/10.1017/S0260210513000065.

60. Brent J. Steele, *Ontological Security in International Relations: Self-Identity and the IR State* (New York: Routledge, 2008), 2.

61. Andrew A. G. Ross, "Realism, Emotion, and Dynamic Allegiances in Global Politics," *International Theory* 5, no. 2 (2013): 295, https://doi.org/10.1017/S175297191300016X.

62. Alexander Wendt, "The State as Person in International Theory," *Review of International Studies* 30, no. 2 (2004): 289–316.

63. Andrew A. G. Ross, *Mixed Emotions: Beyond Fear and Hatred in International Conflict* (Chicago: Chicago University Press, 2014); Emma Hutchison and Roland Bleiker, "Theorizing Emotions in World Politics," *International Theory* 6, no. 3 (2014): 491–514, https://doi.org/10.1017/S1752971914000232; Janice B. Mattern, "On Being Convinced: An Emotional Epistemology of International Relations," *International Theory* 6, no. 3 (2014): 589–94, https://doi.org/10.1017/S1752971914000323.

64. Nicolas Guilhot, "American Katechon: When Political Theology Became International Relations Theory," *Constellations* 17, no. 2 (2010): 224–53; Vassilios Paipais, "Introduction: Political Theologies of the International-the Continued Relevance of Theology in International Relations," *Journal of International Relations and Development* 22, no. 2 (2019): 269–77, https://doi.org/10.1057/s41268-018-0160-2.

65. Thomas, *The Global Resurgence*; Monica Duffy Toft, Daniel Philpott and Timothy Samuel Shah, *God's Century: Resurgent Religion and Global Politics* (New York: W. W. Norton, 2011); Jack L. Snyder, ed., *Religion and International Relations Theory* (New York: Columbia University Press, 2011); Elizabeth Shakman Hurd, *The Politics of Secularism in International Relations* (Princeton, NJ: Princeton University Press, 2008).

66. Charles Taylor, *A Secular Age* (Cambridge, MA: Belknap Press, 2007); Jürgen

Habermas and Joseph Ratzinger, *Dialektik der Säkularisierung. Über Vernunft und Religion*, 7th ed. (Freiburg: Herder, 2005).

67. Jack S. Levy, "International Sources for Interstate and Intrastate War," in *Leashing the Dogs of War: Conflict Management in a Divided World*, ed. Chester A. Crocker (Washington, DC: United States Institute of Peace Press, 2008), 17–38.

68. Nicholas Wheeler, *Saving Strangers: Humanitarian Intervention in International Society* (Oxford: Oxford University Press, 2000).

69. Kenneth Waltz, *Man, the State and War: A Theoretical Analysis* (New York: Columbia University Press, 2001).

70. Michael C. Williams, "Waltz, Realism and Democracy," *International Relations* 23, no. 3 (2009): 328–40; Michael C. Williams, ed., *Realism Reconsidered: The Legacy of Hans Morgenthau in International Relations* (Oxford: Oxford University Press, 2007); Hartmut Behr and Amelia Heath, "Misreading in IR Theory and Ideology Critique: Morgenthau, Waltz and Neo-Realism," *Review of International Studies* 35 (2009): 327–49.

71. Rawi Abdelal, Yoshiko M. Herrera, Alastair Iain Johnston, and Rose McDermott, "Identity as a Variable," *Perspectives on Politics* 4, no. 4 (2006): 695–711.

72. Morgenthau, "The Evil of Politics and the Ethics of Evil," 13.

73. J. S. Barkin, "Constructivism, Realism, and the Variety of Human Natures," in Jacobi and Freyberg-Inan, *Human Beings in International Relations*, 165. See also Robert Powell, "Absolute and Relative Gains in International Relations Theory," *American Political Science Review* 85, no. 4 (1991): 1303–20, https://doi.org/10.2307/1963947.

74. Thomas Hobbes, *The Leviathan* (Cambridge: Cambridge University Press, 1991), 87.

75. Jill Krause and Neil Renwick, eds., *Identities in International Relations* (Basingstoke: St. Martin's Press, 1996); Richard N. Lebow, "Identity and International Relations," *International Relations* 22, no. 4 (2008): 473–92.

76. Monica Duffy Toft, *Securing the Peace: The Durable Settlement of Civil Wars* (Princeton, NJ: Princeton University Press, 2010), 1.

77. Barry Buzan, *From International to World Society? English School Theory and the Social Structure of Globalisation* (Cambridge: Cambridge University Press, 2004).

78. Martin Wight, *International Theory: The Three Traditions* (Leicester: Leicester University Press, 1991), 1.

79. Raymond Aron, *Frieden und Krieg: Eine Theorie der Staatenwelt* (Frankfurt: S. Fischer, 1963), 428.

80. Campbell Craig, *Glimmer of a New Leviathan: Total War in the Realism of Niebuhr, Morgenthau, and Waltz* (New York: Columbia University Press, 2007), 93–116; Hans J. Morgenthau, *Politics in the Twentieth Century* (Chicago: University of Chicago Press, 1971).

81. Girard and Chantre, *Battling to the End*.

82. Raymond Aron, *In Defense of Political Reason: Essays*, ed. Daniel J. Mahoney, (Lanham, MD: Rowman & Littlefield, 1994), 170.

83. Morgenthau, *Scientific Man vs. Power Politics*, 5.

84. Girard and Chantre, *Battling to the End*.

85. Morgenthau, *Scientific Man vs. Power Politics*, 168, 177; A. J. H. Murray, "The Moral Politics of Hans Morgenthau," *Review of Politics* 58, no. 1 (1996): 81–107.

86. Franz L. Neumann, "Approaches of the Study of Power," *Political Science Quarterly*, no. 65, no. 2 (1950): 161–80.

87. Waltz, *Man, the State and War*.

88. Girard and Tincq, "What Is Happening Today Is Mimetic Rivalry on a Global Scale."

89. Robert Gilpin, *The Political Economy of International Relations* (Princeton, NJ: Princeton University Press, 1987).

90. Gideon Rose, "Neoclassical Realism and Theories of Foreign Policy," *World Politics* 51 (October 1998): 144–72; Lobell, Ripsman and Taliaferro, *Neoclassical Realism, the State, and Foreign Policy*; Fareed Zakaria, *The Post-American World* (New York: W. W. Norton, 2008). Similarly, Khanna describes the "rise of the rest" as the phenomena of "How Emerging Powers are Redefining Global Competition." Parag Khanna, *The Second World: How Emerging Powers Are Redefining Global Competition in the Twenty-First Century* (London: Penguin Books, 2008).

91. See also Pankaj Mishra, *Age of Anger: A History of the Present* (New York: Penguin, 2018).

92. Ted R. Gurr, *Why Men Rebel* (Princeton, NJ: Princeton University Press, 1970); Karl Otto Hondrich, *Wieder Krieg* (Frankfurt: Suhrkamp, 2002), 55. See also Hans Magnus Enzensberger, *Aussichten Auf Den Bürgerkrieg* (Frankfurt: Suhrkamp, 1993), 47–48.

93. Girard, *Figuren des Begehrens*, 144.

94. Blok, "The Narcissism of Minor Differences."

95. Carl Schmitt, *The Concept of the Political* (Chicago: University of Chicago Press, 1996).

96. Carl Schmitt, *Ex Captivitate Salus: Erfahrungen Aus Der Zeit 1945/47* (Cologne: Greven Verlag, 1950), 89–90.

97. Samuel P. Huntington, *The Clash of Civilizations and the Remaking of World Order* (New York: Simon & Schuster, 2003).

98. Girard, *Das Ende der Gewalt*, 87.

99. William E. Scheuerman, "Another Hidden Dialogue: Hans Morgenthau and Carl Schmitt," in *Carl Schmitt: The End of Law*, ed. William E. Scheuerman (New York: Rowman & Littlefield, 1999); William E. Scheuerman, "Carl Schmitt and Hans Morgenthau: Realism and Beyond," in Williams, *Realism Reconsidered*. Only in the

second edition of *The Concept of the Political* would Schmitt add the mode of intensity (an idea he took from Morgenthau) to his former dualist conception of friend and foe. It would be too long of a discussion to go into Schmitt's plagiarizing of Morgenthau. For a well-documented impression see Christoph Frei, *Hans J. Morgenthau: Eine intellektuelle Biographie* (Bern: Haupt, 1993), 168–72.

100. Morgenthau, Behr, and Rösch, *The Concept of the Political*, 120.

101. William E. Scheuerman, *Hans Morgenthau: Realism and Beyond* (Cambridge: Polity, 2009), 33.

102. See, for example, Morgenthau, Behr, and Rösch, *The Concept of the Political*, 106.

103. Morgenthau, "The Evil of Politics and the Ethics of Evil," 13; see also Schmitt, *Ex Captivitate Salus*, 89–90.

104. Scheuerman, *Hans Morgenthau*, 34.

105. Hans J. Morgenthau, "Does Disarmament Mean Peace?," in *Arms and Foreign Policy in the Nuclear Age*, ed. Milton J. Rakokove (New York: Oxford University Press, 1972), 422.

106. Paul Sharp, *Diplomatic Theory of International Relations* (Cambridge: Cambridge University Press, 2009), 293.

107. Laurent and Paquet, "Intercultural Relations."

108. Tocqueville, quoted in Laurent and Paquet, "Intercultural Relations," 175–76. See also Palaver, *René Girard's Mimetic Theory*, 61–62.

109. Alexis de Tocqueville, *Democracy in America*, ed. Richard D. Heffner (New York: Mentor Books, 1956), 194. Hartz argued in the same vain for understanding the American democracy. The lacking struggle in American history against feudalism and the therefore primacy of a middle-class fragment of democracy instead, lead to a lack of reactionary or socialist thinking traits. Louis Hartz, *The Liberal Tradition in America: An Interpretation of American Political Thought Since the Revolution* (New York: Harcourt Brace Jovanovich, 1955); Robert Jervis, "Hans Morgenthau, Realism, and the Scientific Study of International Politics," *Social Research* 61, no. 4 (1994): 853–76.

110. Hans J. Morgenthau, *Politics in the Twentieth Century* (Chicago: University of Chicago Press, 1971), 337; Piki Ish-Shalom, "The Triptych of Realism, Elitism, and Conservatism," *International Studies Review* 8 (2006): 441–68.

111. Anthony F. Lang, ed., *Political Theory and International Affairs: Hans J. Morgenthau on Aristotle's 'the Politics'* (Westport, CT: Praeger, 2004).

112. Anthony F. Lang, "Morgenthau, Agency, and Aristotle," in Williams, *Realism Reconsidered*, 30.

113. Morgenthau, "The Evil of Politics and the Ethics of Evil," 13.

114. Morgenthau, Behr and Rösch, *The Concept of the Political*, 49; Robert Schuett, *Political*

Realism, Freud, and Human Nature in International Relations: The Resurrection of the Realist Man (New York: Palgrave Macmillan, 2009).

115. Morgenthau, "The Evil of Politics and the Ethics of Evil," 13.

116. Hans J. Morgenthau, *Science: Servant or Master?* (New York: New American Library, 1972), 31.

117. Morgenthau, *Politics in the Twentieth Century*, 190.

118. Hans J. Morgenthau, "The Significance of Being Alone," n.d., Hans Morgenthau Collection, box 4, folder 6, Leo Baeck Institute.

119. Gil Bailie, *Violence Unveiled: Humanity at the Crossroads* (New York: Crossroad Publ. Co., 1997).

120. Carl Schmitt, *Der Begriff des Politischen*, 2nd ed. (Berlin: Duncker & Humbolt, 2002), 29–30.

121. Hans J. Morgenthau, *Politics Among Nations: The Struggle for Power and Peace*, 5th ed. (New York: Alfred A. Knopf, 1973), 10.

122. Lebow, *The Tragic Vision of Politics*; Chou, "Morgenthau, the Tragic"; Mark Gismondi, "Tragedy, Realism, and Postmodernity: Kulturpessimismus in the Theories of Max Weber, E. H. Carr, Hans J. Morgenthau, and Henry Kissinger," *Diplomacy & Statecraft* 15, no. 3 (2004).

123. Murray, "The Moral Politics of Hans Morgenthau," 106.

124. Morgenthau, *Scientific Man vs. Power Politics*, 209.

125. Kuniyuki Nishimura, "E.H. Carr, Dostoevsky, and the Problem of Irrationality in Modern Europe," *International Relations* 25, no. 1 (2011): 52.

126. One might assume that Kaplan should know better. Especially during his journeys, described in prominent books as *The End of the Earth* or *Balkan Ghosts*, he was interested in how various societies respond to results of state failure by redefining themselves along different, nonmaterial lines such as ethnicity. Robert D. Kaplan, *Warrior Politics: Why Leadership Demands a Pagan Ethos* (New York: Random House, 2002); Robert D. Kaplan, *The Coming Anarchy: Shattering the Dreams of the Post Cold War* (New York: Vintage Books, 2001); Robert D. Kaplan, *The Ends of the Earth: From Togo to Turkmenistan, from Iran to Cambodia; a Journey to the Frontiers of Anarchy* (New York: Vintage Books, 1997); Robert D. Kaplan, *Balkan Ghosts: A Journey Through History* (New York: Picador; Distributed by Holtzbrinck Publishers, 2005). Legend even has it that Bill Clinton's reading of *Balkan Ghosts* is the reason why he did not want to intervene there.

127. Lebow, "Identity and International Relations"; Iver B. Neumann, "Self and Other in International Relations," *European Journal of International Relations* 2, no. 2 (1996): 139–74.

128. Andrew Linklater and Hidemi Suganami, *The English School of International Relations: A Contemporary Reassessment* (Cambridge: Cambridge University Press, 2006), 8. At

the same time as it is called that Cosmopolitanism is a progressive approach toward International Relations, this is also true for Realism. William E. Scheuerman, *The Realist Case for Global Reform* (Cambridge, UK: Polity Press, 2011).

129. Aron, *In Defense of Political Reason*, 170.

130. See also J. Battilana, "Agency and Institutions: The Enabling Role of Individuals' Social Position," *Organization* 13, no. 5 (2006): 653–76.

131. Robert Jackson, *The Global Covenant: Human Conduct in a World of States* (New York: Oxford University Press, 2000).

132. Wendt, "The State as Person in International Theory."

133. Of course, this is not least because mainstream Constructivism exploits a structural explanation of norms diffusion. Alexander Wendt, "The Agent-Structure Problem in International Relations Theory," *International Organization* 41 (1987): 340.

CHAPTER 3. A REALIST MIMETIC VIEW ON RECONCILIATION

1. Daniel Philpott, "Beyond Politics as Usual: Is Reconciliations Compatible with Liberalism?," in *The Politics of Past Evil: Religion, Reconciliation, and the Dilemmas of Transitional Justice*, ed. Daniel Philpott (Notre Dame, IN: University of Notre Dame Press, 2006), 42. This is notwithstanding the fact of the various definitions and understandings of what liberalism actually is. See, for example, Duncan Bell, "What Is Liberalism?," *Political Theory* 42, no. 6 (2014) : 682–715, https://doi.org/10.1177/0090591714535103.

2. Andrew Schaap, "Reconciliation as Ideology and Politics," *Constellations* 15, no. 2 (2008): 249–64, https://doi.org/10.1111/j.1467-8675.2008.00488.x.

3. For the liberal argument see, most prominently, the work of John Rawls, *A Theory of Justice* (Cambridge, MA: Belknap Press, 2005); John Rawls, *Political Liberalism* (New York: Columbia University Press, 2005); Jake Greenblum, "Distributive and Retributive Desert in Rawls," *Journal of Social Philosophy* 41, no. 2 (2010): 169–84, https://doi.org/10.1111/j.1467-9833.2010.01485.x.

4. Samuel P. Huntington, *The Third Wave: Democratization in the Late Twentieth Century* (Norman: University of Oklahoma Press, 1993).

5. For a critical evaluation of the *South African Truth and Reconciliation Commissions* see particularly Judith Renner, "The Local Roots of the Global Politics of Reconciliation: The Articulation of 'Reconciliation' as an Empty Universal in the South African Transition to Democracy," *Millennium: Journal of International Studies* 42, no. 2 (2014): 263–85. Renner makes the case that the installation of those commissions was only due to domestic compromises and hegemonic discourses during the transition period toward democracy. See also Charles Villa-Vicencio, *Walk with Us and Listen: Political Reconciliation in Africa* (Washington, DC: Georgetown University Press,

2009). Mark R. Amstutz, "Restorative Justice, Political Forgiveness, and the Possibility of Political Reconciliation," in Philpott, *The Politics of Past Evil*, 151–88.

6. Kirsten Ainley, "Excesses of Responsibility: The Limits of Law and the Possibilities of Politics," *Ethics & International Affairs* 25, no. 4 (2011): 425.

7. See also Carl Schmitt, *The Concept of the Political* (Chicago: University of Chicago Press, 1996); Chantal Mouffe, *On the Political* (London: Routledge, 2006); Bonnie Honig, *Political Theory and the Displacement of Politics* (Ithaca, NY: Cornell University Press, 1993).

8. Roberto Farneti, *Mimetic Politics: Dyadic Patterns in Global Politics* (East Lansing: Michigan State University Press, 2015), 73–97.

9. Edward Schillebeeckx, ed., *Sacramental Reconciliation* (New York: Herder and Herder, 1971).

10. Daniel Philpott, *Just and Unjust Peace: An Ethic of Political Reconciliation* (New York: Oxford University Press, 2012), 5.

11. Daniel Philpott, "The Justice of Forgiveness," *Journal of Religious Ethics* 41, no. 3 (2013): 400–416, https://doi.org/10.1111/jore.12021.

12. Nicholas Wolterstorff, "The Place of Forgiveness in the Actions of the State," in Philpott, *The Politics of Past Evil*, 92.

13. Andrew Shaap, *Political Reconciliation* (New York: Routledge, 2005), 21. Daniel Philpott, "Beyond Politics as Usual: Is Reconciliations Compatible with Liberalism?," in Philpott, *The Politics of Past Evil*, 20–25.

14. For a basic evaluation of the TRC work see especially Eric Brahm, "Uncovering the Truth: Examining Truth Commission Success and Impact," *International Studies Perspectives* 8, no. 1 (2007): 16–35, https://doi.org/10.1111/j.1528-3585.2007.00267.x; Robert I. Rotberg and Dennis F. Thompson, eds., *Truth V. Justice: The Morality of Truth Commissions* (Princeton, NJ: Princeton University Press, 2000).

15. Christopher A. Hall, "Truth, Pluralism, and Religious Diplomacy: A Christian Dialogical Perspective," in *Religion & Security: The New Nexus in International Relations*, ed. Robert A. Seiple and Dennis R. Hoover (Oxford: Rowman & Littlefield Publishers, 2004), 86.

16. This is an example of the generally under-researched topic of state apologies. See, for example, Mihaela Mihai, "When the State Says 'Sorry': State Apologies as Exemplary Political Judgments," *Journal of Political Philosophy* 21, no. 2 (2013): 200–220, https://doi.org/10.1111/j.1467-9760.2012.00418.x.

17. For an overview of the South African case see Desmond Tutu, *No Future Without Forgiveness* (New York: Image, 1999).

18. Shaap, *Political Reconciliation*, 9.

19. Schmitt, *The Concept of the Political*.

20. Shaap, *Political Reconciliation*, 83.

21. Daniel Philpott, "Beyond Politics as Usual: Is Reconciliations Compatible with Liberalism?," in Philpott, *The Politics of Past Evil*, 12.

22. Given classical liberals' emphasis on punishment, reconciliation's aim toward shalom supposedly will find little support. Daniel Philpott, "Beyond Politics as Usual: Is Reconciliations Compatible with Liberalism?," in Philpott, *The Politics of Past Evil*, 26.

23. Dietrich Bonhoeffer, *The Cost of Discipleship* (New York: Macmillan, 1963), 45–47, 59.

24. Daniel Philpott, "Iraq's Urgent Need for a Reconciliation Ethic," *America*, April 4, 2005, http://americamagazine.org/issue/526/article/iraqs-urgent-need-reconciliation-ethic.

25. Miroslav Volf, "Forgiveness, Reconciliation, and Justice: A Theological Contribution to a More Peaceful Social Environment," *Millennium: Journal of International Studies* 29, no. 3 (2000): 871, https://doi.org/10.1177/03058298000290030601. An alternative form of forgiveness seems to be necessary. It can be found in the Christian faith in that God offers grace nonetheless. There are four main sources of Christian faith that may assemble to form an alternative concept of reconciliation and justice: (1) The primacy of the will to embrace is absolute; it transcends the moral mapping of "good" and "evil," (2) attending to justice as a recondition of actual embrace, (3) the will to embrace as a framework for the search of justice, and (4) embrace as the horizon of the struggle for justice in which telos is always the healing of relationship. Volf, "Forgiveness, Reconciliation, and Justice," 872–75.

26. Susie Linfield, "Trading Truth for Justice? Reflections on South Africa's Truth and Reconciliation Commission," *Boston Review*, 2000, https://bostonreview.net/archives/BR25.3/linfield.html.

27. Lavi Shai, "Crimes of Action, Crimes of Thought: Arendt on Reconciliation, Forgiveness, and Judgment," in *Thinking in Dark Times: Hannah Arendt on Ethics and Politics*, ed. Roger Berkowitz, Jeffrey Katz, and Thomas Keenan (New York: Fordham University Press, 2010).

28. On Arendt, "non-reconciliation," and revenge see particularly Roger Berkowitz, "The Power of Non-Reconciliation: Arendt's Judgment of Adolf Eichmann," *HannahArendt. net* 6, nos. 1/2 (2011), http://www.hannaharendt.net/index.php/han/article/view/11/8; Roger Berkowitz, "The Angry Jew Has Gotten His Revenge," *Philosophical Topics* 39, no. 2 (2011): 1–20, https://doi.org/10.5840/philtopics20113921.

29. Joseph A. Favazza, "Reconciliation: On the Border Between Theological and Political Praxis," *Journal for the Study of Religions & Ideologies* 1, no. 3 (2002): 52–64.

30. Schmitt, *The Concept of the Political*.

31. Kirsten Ainley, "Individual Agency and Responsibility for Atrocity," in *Confronting Evil in International Relations: Ethical Responses to Problems of Moral Agency*, ed. Renée Jeffery (New York: Palgrave Macmillan, 2008); Ainley, "Excesses of Responsibility."

32. Adam Morton, *On Evil* (New York: Routledge, 2004), 125.

33. Hans J. Morgenthau, Hartmut Behr, and Felix Rösch, *The Concept of the Political* (New York: Palgrave Macmillan, 2012), 120. For the "dialogue" between Schmitt and Morgenthau see William E. Scheuerman, "Another Hidden Dialogue: Hans Morgenthau and Carl Schmitt," in *Carl Schmitt: The End of Law*, ed. William E. Scheuerman (New York: Rowman & Littlefield, 1999), 225–51; William E. Scheuerman, "Carl Schmitt and Hans Morgenthau: Realism and Beyond," in *Realism Reconsidered*, ed. Michael C. Williams: *The Legacy of Hans Morgenthau in International Relations* (Oxford: Oxford University Press, 2007), 62–92.

34. Morgenthau, Behr, and Rösch, *The Concept of the Political*, 99.

35. Hans J. Morgenthau, *Scientific Man vs. Power Politics* (Chicago: University of Chicago Press, 1946).

36. Hans J. Morgenthau, "The Evil of Politics and the Ethics of Evil," *Ethics* 56, no. 1 (1945): 13.

37. Hans J. Morgenthau, *Politics Among Nations: The Struggle for Power and Peace*, 5th ed. (New York: Alfred A. Knopf, 1973), 5.

38. Vassilios Paipais, "Between Politics and the Political: Reading Hans J. Morgenthau's Double Critique of Depoliticisation," *Millennium: Journal of International Studies* 42, no. 2 (2014): 369.

39. Morgenthau, "The Evil of Politics and the Ethics of Evil," 11.

40. Ari Kohen, Michael Zanchelli, and Levi Drake, "Personal and Political Reconciliation in Post-Genocide Rwanda," *Social Justice Research* 24, no. 1 (2011): 95, https://doi.org/10.1007/s11211-011-0126-7.

41. Ainley, "Individual Agency and Responsibility for Atrocity."

42. Mervyn Frost, "Constitutive Theory and Moral Accountability: Individuals, Institutions, and Disperse Practices," in *Can Institutions Have Responsibilities? Collective Moral Agency and International Relations*, ed. Toni Erskine (New York: Palgrave Macmillan, 2003), 98.

43. Kohen, Zanchelli, and Drake, "Personal and Political Reconciliation in Post-Genocide Rwanda," 88.

44. See also Hannah Arendt, *The Human Condition*, 2nd ed. (Chicago: University of Chicago Press, 2006); Mouffe, *On the Political*; Honig, *Political Theory and the Displacement of Politics*.

45. Ben Mollov, *Power and Transcendence: Hans J. Morgenthau and the Jewish Experience* (Lanham, MD: Lexington, 2002); Anthony F. Lang, "Morgenthau, Agency, and Aristotle," in Williams, *Realism Reconsidered*; Robert Schuett, *Political Realism, Freud, and Human Nature in International Relations: The Resurrection of the Realist Man* (New York: Palgrave Macmillan, 2009).

46. Despite its comprehensive in-depth knowledge of International Relations and political philosophy, this is also the case in Philpott's *Just and Unjust Peace* where he, at first,

equalizes different streams of Realism and, secondly, equals them with their assumed obsession with power. Philpott, *Just and Unjust Peace*, 75–79.

47. Vern Neufled Redekop and Thomas Ryba, "Introduction: Deep-Rooted Conflict, Reconsiliation, and Mimetic Theory," in *René Girard and Creative Reconciliation*, ed. Vern Neufled Redekop and Thomas Ryba (Lanham: Lexington Books, 2014), 4; Anton Blok, "The Narcissism of Minor Differences," *European Journal of Social Theory* 1, no. 1 (1998): 44–46.

48. Ted R. Gurr, *Why Men Rebel* (Princeton, NJ: Princeton University Press, 1970).

49. T. A. Jacoby, "A Theory of Victimhood: Politics, Conflict and the Construction of Victim-Based Identity," *Millennium: Journal of International Studies* 43, no. 2 (2015): 521. See also James C. Davies, "Towards a Theory of Revolution," *American Sociological Review* 27, no. 1 (1962): 5–19.

50. Blok, "The Narcissism of Minor Differences."

51. Harald Wydra, "Victims and New Wars," *Cambridge Review of International Affairs* 26, no. 1 (2013): 172, https://doi.org/10.1080/09557571.2012.710581.

52. Michael C. Desh, "America's Liberal Illiberalism: The Ideological Origins of Overreaction in U.S. Foreign Policy," *International Security* 32, no. 3 (2007/2008); Ruti G. Teitel, *Humanity's Law* (Oxford: Oxford University Press, 2011).

53. Judith Renner, *Discourse, Normative Change and the Quest for Reconciliation in Global Politics* (Manchester: Manchester University Press, 2013).

54. Nadim Khoury, "Political Reconciliation: With or Without Grand Narratives?" *Constellations* 24, no. 2 (2017): 245–56, https://doi.org/10.1111/1467-8675.12237.

55. Paul Laurent and Gilles Paquet, "Intercultural Relations: A Myrdal—Tocqueville—Girard Interpretative Scheme," *International Political Science Review* 12, no. 3 (1991): 171–83.

56. Karl Otto Hondrich, *Wieder Krieg* (Frankfurt: Suhrkamp, 2002), 55; Davies, "Towards a Theory of Revolution"; Gurr, *Why Men Rebel*.

57. Hans Magnus Enzensberger, *Civil War* (London: Granta Books, 1994), 39.

58. Philpott, *Just and Unjust Peace*, 72.

59. René Girard and Benoît Chantre, *Battling to the End: Conversations with Benoît Chantre* (East Lansing: Michigan State University Press, 2010), 42.

60. See, for example, Joshua S. Goldstein, *Winning the War on War: The Decline of Armed Conflict Worldwide* (New York: Dutton, 2011).

61. Enzensberger, *Civil War*. On urban "civic" war, see particularly J. Beall, T. Goodfellow, and D. Rodgers, "Cities and Conflict in Fragile States in the Developing World," *Urban Studies* 50, no. 15 (2013): 1–19, https://doi.org/10.1177/0042098013487775.

62. Frantz Fanon and Richard Philcox, *The Wretched of the Earth* (New York: Grove Press, 2004).

63. Scott Atran, *Talking to the Enemy: Violent Extremism, Sacred Values, and What It Means to Be Human* (London: Penguin, 2011), 358.

64. Wydra, "Victims and New Wars," 176.

65. Hannah Arendt, *Eichmann in Jerusalem: Ein Bericht von der Banalität des Bösen* (Munich: Piper, 2006).

66. Donald W. Shriver, *An Ethic for Enemies: Forgiveness in Politics* (New York: Oxford University Press, 1998).

67. See, for example the focus in Jack Snyder and Leslie Vinjamuri, "Trials and Errors: Principle and Pragmatism in Strategies of International Justice," *International Security* 28, no. 3 (2004): 5–44, https://doi.org/10.1162/016228803773100066; Kathryn Sikkink, *The Justice Cascade: How Human Rights Prosecutions Are Changing World Politics* (New York: W. W. Norton 2011).

68. Wydra, "Victims and New Wars," 176.

69. Shriver, *An Ethic for Enemies*, 63.

70. Cited in Shriver, *An Ethic for Enemies*, 64–65.

71. Sandor Goodhart and Yubraj Aryal, "The Self and Other People," *Journal of Philosophy: A Cross-Disciplinary Inquiry* 7, no. 16 (2011): 14–25, https://doi.org/10.5840/jphilnepal201171613; Rowan Williams, "Foreword," in *Can We Survive Our Origins? Readings in Rene Girard's Theory of Violence and the Sacred*, ed. Pierpaolo Antonello and Paul Gifford (East Lansing: Michigan State University Press, 2015), xi–xvi.

CHAPTER 4. DAG HAMMARSKJÖLD—
INTERNATIONAL CIVIL SERVICE AND MIMESIS

1. For a basic overview of the life and work of Dag Hammarskjöld, see "Dag Hammarskjöld: The UN Years," United Nations, last modified July 26, 2018, http://www.un.org/depts/dhl/dag/index.html. See also Brian Urquhart, *Hammarskjöld* (New York: Norton, 1994); Gustav Aulen, *Dag Hammarskjöld's White Book: An Analysis of Markings* (London: SPCK, 1970); Roger Lipsey, *Hammarskjöld: A Life* (Ann Arbor: University of Michigan Press, 2013); Manuel Fröhlich, *Political Ethics and the United Nations: Dag Hammarskjöld as Secretary-General* (New York: Routledge, 2008). Hammarskjöld earned the respect for his work already during his period at the OEECD. Nonetheless, secretary-general Hammarskjöld faced insoluble problems while in office. Brian Urquhart, "International Peace and Security: Thoughts on the Twentieth Anniversary of Dag Hammarskjöld's Death," *Foreign Affairs* 60, no. 1 (1981): 1–16.

2. There are many editions and translations of *Markings* now. See, for example, Dag Hammarskjöld, *Markings*, trans. by Leif Sjöberg and W. H. Auden (New York: Vintage Spiritual Classics, 2006); Seven Stolpe, *Dag Hammarskjöld: A Spiritual Portrait* (New York: Charles Scribner's Sons, 1966); K. G. Hammar, "Dag Hammarskjöld and

Markings," in *The Adventure of Peace: Dag Hammarskjöld and the Future of the UN*, ed. Sten Ask and Mark-Jungkoist (New York: Palgrave Macmillan, 2005), 110–25.

3. Stolpe, *Dag Hammarskjöld*, 6.

4. Alynna J. Lyon, "The UN Charter, the New Testament, and the Psalms: The Moral Authority of Dag Hammarskjöld," in *The UN Secretary-General and Moral Authority*, ed. Kent J. Kille (Washington, DC: Georgetown University Press, 2007), 111, 132. Filippo Dionigi, "Dag Hammarskjöld's Religiosity and Norms Entrepreneurship: A Post-Secular Perspective," *Politics and Religion* 9, no. 1 (2016): 162–86.

5. Daniel L. Byman and Kenneth M. Pollack, "Let Us Now Praise Great Man: Bringing the Statesman Back In," *International Security* 25, no. 4 (2001): 107–46; Kille, *The UN Secretary-General and Moral Authority*; Brian Urquhart, "Learning from Hammarskjöld," *New York Times*, September 16, 2011, http://www.nytimes.com/2011/09/17/opinion/learning-from-hammarskjold.html; Robert A. Isaak, *Individuals and World Politics* (North Scituate, MA: Duxbury Press, 1975), 201–22.

6. Kille, *The UN Secretary-General and Moral Authority*, 11.

7. Hammarskjöld, *Markings*, 122.

8. Costas M. Constantinou, "Human Diplomacy and Spirituality," *Clingendael Discussion Paper in Diplomacy*, no. 103 (2006): 16, https://www.clingendael.org/publication/human-diplomacy-and-spirituality.

9. Constantinou, "Human Diplomacy and Spirituality," 17.

10. James Mayall, "Introduction," in *The Diplomatic Corps as an Institution of International Society*, ed. Paul Sharp and Geoffrey Wiseman (London: Palgrave Macmillan, 2007), 9.

11. Anthony F. Lang Jr., "Phronesis, Morgenthau and Diplomacy," E-International Relations, November 7, 2013, http://www.e-ir.info/2013/11/07/phronesis-morgenthau-and-diplomacy/#_ftn5.

12. Kent J. Kille, "Moral Authority and the UN Secretary-General's Ethical Framework," in Kille, *The UN Secretary-General and Moral Authority*, 20.

13. Bernard McGinn, *The Foundations of Christian Mysticism: The Presence of God: A History of Western Christian Mysticism* (New York: Crossroad, 1991), 1, xvii.

14. Fred Dallmayr, "A Global Spiritual Resurgence? On Christian and Islamic Spiritualities," in *Religion in International Relations: The Return from Exile*, ed. Pavlos a. P. F. Hatzopoulos (New York: Palgrave Macmillan, 2003), 215.

15. Alynna J. Lyon, "The UN Charter, the New Testament, and the Psalms: The Moral Authority of Dag Hammarskjöld," in Kille, *The UN Secretary-General and Moral Authority*, 117.

16. See also Ben Mollov, Ephraim Meir, and Chaim Lavie, "An Integrated Strategy for Peacebuilding: Judaic Approaches," *Die Friedenswarte. Journal of International Peace and Organization* 82, nos. 2–3 (2007): 141; Lou Marin, "Can We Save True Dialogue

in an Age of Mistrust? The Encounter of Dag Hammarskjöld and Martin Buber," *Critical Currents* 8 (2010).

17. Dallmayr, "A Global Spiritual Resurgence?" 218.

18. Wilder Foote, ed., *Dag Hammarskjöld: Servant of Peace; A Selection of His Speeches and Statements* (New York: Harper & Row, 1962), 27.

19. Foote, *Dag Hammarskjöld*, 24.

20. This is a parallel to the concern of former Pope Benedict XVI. See, for example, Jürgen Habermas and Joseph Ratzinger, *Dialektik der Säkularisierung: Über Vernunft und Religion*, 7th ed. (Freiburg: Herder, 2005).

21. Richard P. Hardy, "Hammarskjöld, the Mystic," *Ephemerides Carmelitiacae* 29 (1978): 271.

22. Dallmayr, "A Global Spiritual Resurgence?" 218.

23. Dallmayr, "A Global Spiritual Resurgence?" 218.

24. Hammarskjöld, *Markings*, 57.

25. Alynna J. Lyon, "The UN Charter, the New Testament, and the Psalms: The Moral Authority of Dag Hammarskjöld," in Kille, *The UN Secretary-General and Moral Authority*, 119.

26. Dorothy V. Jones, "The World Outlook of Dag Hammarskjöld," in *Ethics and Statecraft: The Moral Dimension of International Affairs*, ed. Cathal J. Nolan, 2nd ed. (Westport, CT: Praeger, 2004), 134.

27. See, for example, Edward Johnson, "The British and the 1960 Soviet Attack on the Office of United Nations Secretary-General," *Diplomacy & Statecraft* 14, no. 1 (2003): 79–102.

28. Jebb Gladwyn, *The Memoirs of Lord Gladwyn* (New York: Weybright Talley, 1972), 257.

29. Gladwyn, *The Memoirs of Lord Gladwyn*, 258.

30. Joseph P. Lash, *Dag Hammarskjöld: Custodian of the Bushfire Peace* (Garden City, NY: Doubleday & Co., 1961), 203.

31. Kent J. Kille, "Introduction," in Kille, *The UN Secretary-General and Moral Authority*, 1.

32. Hammarskjöld, *Markings*, 65.

33. Chris Brown, "The 'Practice Turn,' Phronesis and Classical Realism: Towards a Phronetic International Political Theory?" *Millennium: Journal of International Studies* 40, no. 3 (2012): 439–56.

34. Lash, *Dag Hammarskjöld*, 211.

35. Brian Urquhart, "The Secretary-General: Why Dag Hammarskjöld," in Ask and Mark-Jungkoist, *The Adventure of Peace*, 21.

36. Paul Sharp, "Herbert Butterfield, the English School and the Civilizing Virtues of Diplomacy," *International Affairs* 9, no. 4 (2003): 877.

37. Sharp, "Herbert Butterfield, the English School and the Civilizing Virtues of Diplomacy," 862.

38. Herbert Butterfield, *History and Human Relations* (London: HarperCollins, 1951), 26.

39. Ali A. Mazrui, *Cultural Forces in World Politics* (1990; Oxford: J. Currey, 2000), 21–24.

40. Pope John Paul II, "No Peace Without Justice: No Justice Without Forgiveness," Message for the Celebration of the World Day of Peace, January 1, 2002, http://www.vatican.va/holy_father/john_paul_ii/messages/peace/documents/hf_jp-ii_mes_20011211_xxxv-world-day-for-peace_en.html.

41. Manuel Fröhlich, *Dag Hammarskjöld und die Vereinten Nationen: Die politische Ethik Des Generalsekretärs* (Paderborn: Schöning, 2002), 132–33.

42. Urquhart, "International Peace and Security," 3.

43. Barry Buzan, *From International to World Society? English School Theory and the Social Structure of Globalisation* (Cambridge: Cambridge University Press, 2004), 7. See also Andrew Linklater and Hidemi Suganami, *The English School of International Relations: A Contemporary Reassessment* (Cambridge: Cambridge University Press, 2006).

44. Kent J. Kille, "The Secular Pope: Insights on the UN Secretary-General and Moral Authority," in Kille, *The UN Secretary-General and Moral Authority*. Pope Pius XII called the United Nations' secretary-general as his secular counterpart. Lipsey, *Hammarskjold*, 153. Hammarskjöld did not reject this terminology.

45. Buzan, *From International to World Society?*, 7.

46. Robert Jackson, *The Global Covenant: Human Conduct in a World of States* (New York: Oxford University Press, 2000).

47. The "resolution of the Suez Canal crisis introduced the word *peacekeeping* into the lexicon of the United Nations." Alynna J. Lyon, "The UN Charter, the New Testament, and the Psalms: The Moral Authority of Dag Hammarskjöld," in Kille, *The UN Secretary-General and Moral Authority*, 130. See also Kaladharan M. G. Nayar, "Dag Hammarskjöld and U Thant: The Evolution of Their Offices," *Case Western Reserve Journal of International Law* 36 (1974): 54.

48. Lipsey, *Hammarskjold*, 155, 311.

49. Hammarskjöld, *Markings*, 110.

50. Fröhlich, *Dag Hammarskjöld und die Vereinten Nationen*, 343.

51. Connor Cruise O'Brien, "Common Sense and Unjust Wars," in *Religion and*

International Affairs, ed. Jeffrey Rose and Michael Ignatieff (Toronto: Anansi, 1968), 21.

52. Dag Hammarskjöld, "Remarks at United Nations Day Concert, New York, October 24, 1960," http://www.un.org/depts/dhl/dag/undayconcert.htm.

53. Kurt Waldheim, "Dag Hammarskjöld and the Office of United Nations Secretary-General," in *Dag Hammarskjöld Revisited: The UN Secretary-General as a Force in World Politics*, ed. Robert S. Jordan (Durham, NC: Carolina Academic Press, 1983), 16.

54. Dorothy V. Jones, "The Example of Dag Hammarskjöld: Style and Effectiveness at the UN," *Christian Century* 111, no. 32 (1994): 1047–50.

55. United Nations Chronicle, "Dag Hammarskjöld: 'Virtuoso of Multilateral Diplomacy,'" *United Nations Chronicle* 28, no. 3 (1991): 74–76.

56. Alynna J. Lyon, "The UN Charter, the New Testament, and the Psalms: The Moral Authority of Dag Hammarskjöld," in Kille, *The UN Secretary-General and Moral Authority*, 133.

57. Hammarskjöld, *Markings*, 67.

58. Foote, *Dag Hammarskjöld*, 348.

59. Foote, *Dag Hammarskjöld*, 124.

60. Lyon, "The UN Charter," 121.

61. Lyon, "The UN Charter," 117–18.

62. Dorothy V. Jones, "Seeking Balance: The Secretary-General as Normative Negotiator," in Kille, *The UN Secretary-General and Moral Authority*, 61.

63. Mollov, Meir and Lavie, "An Integrated Strategy for Peacebuilding," 154.

64. Mollov, Meir and Lavie, "An Integrated Strategy for Peacebuilding," 154.

65. Jones, "The Example of Dag Hammarskjöld," 1050. Moreover, there is a "deep connection officeholders felt with the charter. They often engaged the charter with an almost religious reverence as a sacred text and perceived themselves as the embodiment of the charter and its ethical code. Individual officeholders may have interpreted the exact dictates of the charter in the light of their own ethical framework . . . Yet, in many ways, from the perspective of the secretaries-general the charter already provides a global ethic for the international community, and they have done their best to uphold the document accordingly." Kent J. Kille, "The Secular Pope: Insights on the UN Secretary-General and Moral Authority," in Kille, *The UN Secretary-General and Moral Authority*, 352.

66. Jones, "The World Outlook of Dag Hammarskjöld," 143.

67. René Girard, *The Scapegoat* (Baltimore: Johns Hopkins University Press, 1986); René Girard, *Violence and the Sacred* (Baltimore: Johns Hopkins University Press, 1979).

68. Plato, *The Republic*, ed. G. R. F. Ferraris, trans. T. Griffith (Cambridge: Cambridge University Press, 2000), 205; Augustine, *Concerning the City of God Against the Pagans*, trans. H. Bettension (London: Penguin Books, 2003), 324.

69. Hammarskjöld, *Markings*, 140.

70. Hammarskjöld, *Markings*, 83.

71. Miroslav Volf, *Exclusion and Embrace: A Theological Exploration of Identity, Otherness, and Reconciliation* (Nashville: Abingdon Press, 1996).

72. Eric Voegelin, *Political Religions* (Lewiston, NY: E. Mellen Press, 1986); Eric Voegelin, *Der Gottesmord: Zur Genese und Gestalt der modernen politischen Gnosis* (Munich: Fink, 1999), 119.

73. Hammarskjöld, *Markings*, 149.

74. Lyon, "The UN Charter," 132, 134.

75. Conor Cruise O'Brien, *To Katanga and Back* (New York: Simon & Schuster, 1962), 14–15. See also Ole Jacob Sending, *The Politics of Expertise: Competing for Authority in Global Governance* (Ann Arbor: University of Michigan Press, 2015), 47–53.

76. Costas M. Constantinou, "Human Diplomacy and Spirituality," 17.

77. Hammarskjöld, *Markings*, 90.

78. Hammarskjöld, *Markings*, 156.

79. Elif Shafak, "Our Compass," *New York Times*, November 27, 2013, https://www.nytimes.com/2013/11/28/opinion/our-compass.html?pagewanted=3&_r=0.

80. Herbert Butterfield, *Christianity, Diplomacy and War* (New York: Abingdon-Cokesbury Press, 1954), 12.

81. Urquhart, "Learning from Hammarskjöld."

82. See, for example, Oskar Schachter, "Dag Hammarskjöld and the Relation of Law to Politics," *The American Journal of International Law* 56, no. 1 (1962): 4.

CHAPTER 5. TOWARD COMPETITION WITHOUT VIOLENCE

1. Margaret Truman, *Where the Buck Stops: The Personal and Private Writings of Harry S. Truman* (New York: Warner Books, 1990), 202.

2. Hans J. Morgenthau, *Politics Among Nations: The Struggle for Power and Peace*, 5th ed. (New York: Alfred A. Knopf, 1973), 229.

3. *Fury*, dir. David Ayer (Los Angeles: Columbia Pictures, 2014).

4. Thomas Hobbes, *The Leviathan* (Cambridge: Cambridge University Press, 1991).

5. René Girard, *Violence and the Sacred* (Baltimore: Johns Hopkins University Press, 1979), 49; Paul Laurent and Gilles Paquet, "Intercultural Relations: A

Myrdal—Tocqueville—Girard Interpretative Scheme," *International Political Science Review* 12, no. 3 (1991): 171–83.

6. Scott Atran, *Talking to the Enemy: Violent Extremism, Sacred Values, and What It Means to Be Human* (London: Penguin, 2011), 482.

7. Kai Bird and Martin J. Sherwin, *American Prometheus: The Triumph and Tragedy of J. Robert Oppenheimer* (London: Atlantic, 2009), 426.

8. Laurent and Paquet, "Intercultural Relations"; Pankaj Mishra, *Age of Anger: A History of the Present* (New York: Penguin, 2018).

9. Hans J. Morgenthau, Hartmut Behr, and Felix Rösch, *The Concept of the Political* (New York: Palgrave Macmillan, 2012), 120.

10. On the relative, relational and social quality of power see J. Samuel Barkin, *Realist Constructivism: Rethinking International Relations Theory* (Cambridge: Cambridge University Press, 2010), 18–20.

11. Johan Galtung, *Strukturelle Gewalt: Beiträge zur Friedens- und Konfliktforschung* (Reinbek bei Hamburg: Rowohlt, 1975).

12. Michael C. Williams, "Why Ideas Matter in International Relations: Hans Morgenthau, Classical Realism, and the Moral Construction of Power Politics," *International Organization* 58, no. 4 (2004): 644, https://doi.org/10.1017/S0020818304040202.

13. William Bain, "Deconfusing Morgenthau: Moral Inquiry and Classical Realism Reconsidered," *Review of International Studies* 26, no. 3 (2000): 445–64.

14. Jonathan Kirshner, "The Economic Sins of Modern IR Theory and the Classical Realist Alternative," *World Politics* 67, no. 1 (2014): 155–83, https://doi.org/10.1017/S0043887114000318. It is thus that the English School is commonly associated with structural approaches as criticized. See, for example, Barry Buzan, *From International to World Society? English School Theory and the Social Structure of Globalisation* (Cambridge: Cambridge University Press, 2004); Martha Finnemore, "Exporting the English School?" *Review of International Studies* 27 (2001): 509–13.

15. Martti Koskenniemi, *The Gentle Civilizer of Nations: The Rise and Fall of International Law, 1870–1960* (Cambridge: Cambridge University Press, 2002), 454.

16. Richard Ned Lebow, *The Tragic Vision of Politics: Ethics, Interests and Orders* (Cambridge: Cambridge University Press, 2003), 224.

17. Lebow, *The Tragic Vision of Politics*, 226.

18. Hans J. Morgenthau, "The Evil of Politics and the Ethics of Evil," *Ethics* 56, no. 1 (1945): 13.

19. Mitchell Reiss, *Bridled Ambition: Why Countries Constrain Their Nuclear Capabilities* (Washington, DC: Woodrow Wilson Center Press, 1995).

20. William Wallace, "Truth and Power, Monks and Technocrats: Theory and Practice in International Relations," *Review of International Studies* 22 (1996): 317n54.

21. See also Robert Jackson, *The Global Covenant: Human Conduct in a World of States* (New York: Oxford University Press, 2000).

22. Meic Pearse, *Why the Rest Hates the West: Understanding the Roots of Global Rage* (Downers Grove, IL: InterVarsity Press, 2004).

23. See, for example, Gordon Adams and Shoon K. Murray, eds., *Mission Creep: The Militarization of US Foreign Policy?* (Washington, DC: Georgetown University Press, 2014).

24. Kerstin Fisk and Jennifer M. Ramos, "Actions Speak Louder Than Words: Preventive Self-Defense as a Cascading Norm," *International Studies Perspectives* 15, no. 2 (2013): 163–85, https://doi.org/10.1111/insp.12013; Ian Hurd, "'If I Had a Rocket Launcher': Self-Defense and Forever War in International Law," *Houston Law Review* 56, no. 4 (2019): 821–39.

25. John J. Mearsheimer, "Why the Ukraine Crisis Is the West's Fault," *Foreign Affairs* 93, no. 5 (2014): 1–12.

26. Henry Kissinger, *World Order: Reflections on the Character of Nations and the Course of History* (London: Alan Lane an Imprint of Penguin Books, 2014), 6.

27. See, for example, Peter Wallensteen, *Quality Peace: Strategic Peacebuilding and World Order* (New York: Oxford University Press, 2015), 2.

28. Reid J. Epstein, "Kerry: Russia Behaving Like It's the 19th Century," *Politico*, March 2, 2014, https://www.politico.com/blogs/politico-now/2014/03/kerry-russia-behaving-like-its-the-19th-century-184280.

29. Sinn Féin, the political arm of the Irish Republican Army (IRA) means "we ourselves."

30. "How Qatar Came to Host the Taliban," BBC News, June 22, 2013, https://www.bbc.com/news/world-asia-23007401; Paul Sharp, "Mullah Zaeef and Taliban Diplomacy: An English School Approach," *Review of International Studies* 29 (2003): 481–98, https://doi.org/10.1017/S0260210503004819.

31. Simone M. Friis, "'Beyond Anything We Have Ever Seen': Beheading Videos and the Visibility of Violence in the War Against ISIS," *International Affairs* 91 (2015): 727, https://doi.org/10.1111/1468-2346.12341. See also Simone M. Friis, "'Behead, Burn, Crucify, Crush': Theorizing the Islamic State's Public Displays of Violence," *European Journal of International Relations* 24 (2017): 243–67, https://doi.org/10.1177/1354066117714416.

32. Ward Thomas, *The Ethics of Destruction: Norms and Force in International Relations* (Ithaca, NY: Cornell University Press, 2001).

33. Rebecca Sanders, *Plausible Legality: Legal Culture and Political Imperative in the Global War on Terror* (New York: Oxford University Press, 2018); see also Judith Nisse Shklar,

Legalism: Law, Morals, and Political Trials (Cambridge, MA: Harvard University Press, 1964).

34. Michael C. Williams, "What Is the National Interest? The Neoconservative Challenge in IR Theory," *The European Journal of International Relations* 11, no. 3 (2005): 307–37; Greg Russel, "Hans J. Morgenthau and the National Interest," *Society in Transition* 31, no. 2 (1994): 80–84.

35. Kirsten Ainley, "Excesses of Responsibility: The Limits of Law and the Possibilities of Politics," *Ethics & International Affairs* 25, no. 4 (2011): 407–31.

36. Kirsten Ainley, "The Responsibility to Protect and the International Criminal Court: Counteracting the Crisis," *International Affairs* 91, no. 1 (2015): 37–54, https://doi.org/10.1111/1468-2346.12185.

37. William A. Johnsen, "Geoffrey Hill, René Girard, and the Logic of Sacrifice," *Religion and the Arts* 16, no. 5 (2012): 577, https://doi.org/10.1163/15685292-12341240.

38. Ainley, "Excesses of Responsibility," 410.

39. Ainley, "Excesses of Responsibility," 412.

40. Johnsen, "Geoffrey Hill, René Girard, and the Logic of Sacrifice," 576–77.

41. See, for example, Anne-Marie Slaughter's call for no-kill zones in Syria. Anne-Marie Slaughter, "How to Halt the Butchery in Syria," *New York Times*, February 23, 2012, http://www.nytimes.com/2012/02/24/opinion/how-to-halt-the-butchery-in-syria.html?_r=1.

42. Amitai Etzioni, "The Democratisation Mirage," *Survival* 57, no. 4 (2015): 139–56, https://doi.org/10.1080/00396338.2015.1068570.

43. See also David Rieff, *A Bed for the Night: Humanitarianism in Crisis* (London: Vintage, 2002).

44. Rowan Williams, "Foreword," in *Can We Survive Our Origins? Readings in Rene Girard's Theory of Violence and the Sacred*, ed. Pierpaolo Antonello and Paul Gifford (East Lansing: Michigan State University Press, 2015), xiv.

45. Richard Shapcott, "IR as Practical Philosophy: Defining a 'Classical Approach,'" *British Journal of Politics and International Relations* 6, no. 3 (2004): 274.

46. J. Tir and P. F. Diehl, "Demographic Pressure and Interstate Conflict: Linking Population Growth and Density to Militarized Disputes and Wars, 1930–89," *Journal of Peace Research* 35, no. 3 (1998): 319–39, https://doi.org/10.1177/0022343398035003004.

47. Robert Muggah, *Researching the Urban Dilemma: Urbanization, Poverty and Violence* (Ottawa: International Development Research Centre, 2012); A. Hasan, "Can Urban Density Be Made to Work for Everyone? Exploring Options for Karachi's Low- and Lower-Middle-Class Settlements," *Environment and Urbanization* 22, no. 1 (2010): 267–68, https://doi.org/10.1177/0956247810364116; O. Jütersonke, R. Muggah, and D. Rodgers, "Gangs, Urban Violence, and Security Interventions

in Central America," *Security Dialogue* 40, nos. 4–5 (2009): 373–97, https://doi.
org/10.1177/0967010609343298; Alexandre Marc and Alys M. Willman, *Violence
in the City: Understanding and Supporting Community Responses to Urban Violence*
(Washington, DC: World Bank, 2010).

48. Natalie Brender, "Researching the Urban Dilemma: Urbanization, Poverty and
Violence," http://hasow.org/uploads/trabalhos/99/doc/852753071.pdf, 7. Unrest
and riots in suburbs are also a probable indicator for Samuel Huntington's thesis of
a too-slow adjustment of political order toward changing societies, placing emphasis
on factors such as urbanization rather than economic change. Clifford Deaton, "The
Revolution Will Not Be Occupied: Theorizing Urban Revolutionary Movements in
Tehran, Prague, and Paris," *Territory, Politics, Governance* 3, no. 2 (2015): 205–26,
https://doi.org/10.1080/21622671.2014.945473; Mustafa Dike, "Disruptive Politics,"
Urban Studies 54, no. 1 (2017): 49–54, https://doi.org/10.1177/0042098016671476.

49. Colin McFarlane, "The Geographies of Urban Density," *Progress in Human Geography*
40, no. 5 (2016): 644, https://doi.org/10.1177/0309132515608694. "If key
sociospatial categories have been the foci of this politics—slum, suburb, skyscraper,
city centre, the socially mixed city—new techniques and developments such as those
around new urbanism, digital urbanism, and activist occupation have both shifted
how these are understood and forced new questions about the future of density in and
between cities. And yet, the political conceptions and uses of density have often been
in the background of urban analysis." McFarlane, "The Geographies of Urban Density,"
644. See also Ash Amin and Nigel Thrift, *Seeing Like a City* (Cambridge, UK: Polity
Press, 2016).

50. Mustafa Dikec, *Urban Rage: The Revolt of the Excluded* (New Haven, CT: Yale
University Press, 2018).

51. T. A. Jacoby, "A Theory of Victimhood: Politics, Conflict and the Construction of
Victim-Based Identity," *Millennium: Journal of International Studies* 43, no. 2 (2015):
521; Robert Forsyth Worth, *A Rage for Order: The Middle East in Turmoil, from Tahrir
Square to ISIS* (New York: Farrar, Straus and Giroux, 2016).

52. Jenny Edkins and Maja Zehfuss, "Generalising the International," *Review of
International Studies* 31, no. 3 (2005): 471.

53. Martin Coward, *Urbicide: The Politics of Urban Destruction* (London: Routledge,
2009), 128.

54. Pierre Bourdieu, *Distinction: A Social Critique of the Judgement of Taste*, trans. Richard
Nice (London: Routledge, 1984), 479. Sigmund Freud called this the "Narcissism of
minor differences." Anton Blok, "The Narcissism of Minor Differences," *European
Journal of Social Theory* 1, no. 1 (1998): 33–56.

55. Laurent and Paquet, "Intercultural Relations."

56. Ted R. Gurr, *Why Men Rebel* (Princeton, NJ: Princeton University Press, 1970); Karl
Otto Hondrich, *Wieder Krieg* (Frankfurt: Suhrkamp, 2002), 55. See also Hans Magnus
Enzensberger, *Aussichten auf den Bürgerkrieg* (Frankfurt: Suhrkamp, 1993), 47–48.

57. Morgenthau, "The Evil of Politics and the Ethics of Evil," 13.

58. Thomas L. Friedman, *The World Is Flat: The Globalized World in the Twenty-First Century* (London: Penguin Books, 2006).

59. Laurent and Paquet, "Intercultural Relations."

60. Benjamin R. Barber, *Jihad vs. McWorld* (New York: Times Books, 1995); Elisabetta Brighi, "The Globalisation of Resentment: Failure, Denial and Violence in World Politics," *Millennium: Journal of International Studies* 44, no. 3 (2016): 411–32; Mishra, *Age of Anger*.

61. Fareed Zakaria, *The Post-American World: Release 2.0* (New York: W. W. Norton, 2011), 35.

62. Jacoby, "A Theory of Victimhood," 521. See also Gurr, *Why Men Rebel*.

63. Henrik Urdal and Kristian Hoelscher, "Explaining Urban Social Disorder and Violence: An Empirical Study of Event Data from Asian and Sub-Saharan African Cities," *International Interactions* 38, no. 4 (2012): 512–28, https://doi.org/10.1080/0 3050629.2012.697427.

64. Joan Nelson, "The Urban Poor: Disruption or Political Integration in Third World Cities?," *World Politics* 22, no. 3 (1970): 395; Clionadh Raleigh, "Urban Violence Patterns Across African States," *International Studies Review* 17, no. 1 (2015): 90–106, https://doi.org/10.1111/misr.12206.

65. J. Beall, T. Goodfellow, and D. Rodgers, "Cities and Conflict in Fragile States in the Developing World," *Urban Studies* 50, no. 15 (2013): 8, https://doi.org/10.1177/0042098013487775.

66. Beall, Goodfellow, and Rodgers, "Cities and Conflict in Fragile States in the Developing World," 5.

67. Martin Coward, "Network-Centric Violence, Critical Infrastructure and the Urbanization of Security," *Security Dialogue* 40, nos. 4–5 (2009): 399–418, https://doi.org/10.1177/0967010609342879.

68. Saskia Sassen, "The Global Street: Making the Political," *Globalizations* 8, no. 5 (2011): 574, https://doi.org/10.1080/14747731.2011.622458.

69. Beall, Goodfellow, and Rodgers, "Cities and Conflict in Fragile States in the Developing World," 11.

70. Charles Tilly, "War Making and State Making as Organized Crime," in *Bringing the State Back in*, ed. Peter B. Evans, Dietrich Rueschemeyer, and Theda Skocpol (Cambridge: Cambridge University Press, 1985), 169–91. Enzensberger even holds that violence is an elementary part of human life and civil war the "primary form of war." Hans Magnus Enzensberger, *Civil War* (London: Granta Books, 1994), 11.

71. James C. Scott, *Seeing Like a State: How Certain Schemes to Improve the Human Condition Have Failed* (New Haven, CT: Yale University Press, 1998), 92.

72. Scott, *Seeing Like a State*, 144; Doug Saunders, *Arrival City: The Final Migration and Our Next World* (Toronto: Knopf Canada, 2010); Mike Davis, *Planet of Slums* (New York: Verso, 2006); Ricky Burdett, "Designing Urban Democracy: Mapping Scales of Urban Identity," *Public Culture* 25, no. 2 (2013): 349–67, https://doi.org/10.1215/08992363-2020638.

73. Marc Angélil and Cary Siress, "The Paris Banlieue: Peripheries of Inequity," *Journal of International Affairs* 65, no. 2 (2012): 57–67; Mélina Germes and Georg Glasze, "Die Banlieus als Gegenorte der République: Eine Diskursanalyse neuer Sicherheitspolitiken in den Vorstädten Frankreichs," *Geographica Helvetica* 65, no. 3 (2010): 217–28. Not terrorism, "but what has been done under the mantel of counter-terrorism, has had a significant effect on cities." Peter Marcuse, "The 'War on Terrorism' and Life in Cities after September 11, 2001," in *Cities, War, and Terrorism: Towards an Urban Geopolitics*, ed. Stephen Graham (Malden, MA: Blackwell Publishing, 2004), 263–75, 263.

74. P. H. Liotta and James F. Miskel, "The 'Mega-Eights': Urban Leviathans and International Instability," *Orbis* 53, no. 4 (2009): 648–49, https://doi.org/10.1016/j.orbis.2009.07.003.

75. Saskia Sassen, "Urban Capabilities," *Journal of International Affairs* 65, no. 2 (2012): 85–95.

76. René Girard, *Ich sah den Satan vom Himmel fallen wie einen Blitz: Eine kritische Apologie Des Christentums* (Munich: Hanser, 2002), 23; René Girard, *Deceit, Desire, and the Novel: Self and Other in Literary Structure* (Baltimore: Johns Hopkins University Press, 1976); René Girard, *Das Ende der Gewalt: Analyse des Menschheitsverhängnisses* (Freiburg im Breisgau: Herder, 1983).

77. William E. Scheuerman, "The Realist Revival in Political Philosophy, or: Why New Is Not Always Improved," *International Politics* 50, no. 6 (2013): 798–814.

78. Morgenthau, Behr, and Rösch, *The Concept of the Political*, 99.

79. Hedley Bull, "International Theory: The Case for a Classical Approach," *World Politics* 18, no. 3 (1966): 361–77.

80. Shapcott, "IR as Practical Philosophy"; Chris Brown, "The 'Practice Turn,' Phronesis and Classical Realism: Towards a Phronetic International Political Theory?" *Millennium: Journal of International Studies* 40, no. 3 (2012): 439–56.

81. Martin Wight, *International Theory: The Three Traditions* (Leicester: Leicester University Press, 1991), 1.

82. Raymond Aron, *In Defense of Political Reason: Essays*, ed. Daniel J. Mahoney (Lanham, MD: Rowman & Littlefield, 1994), 170.

83. Sandor Goodhart and Yubraj Aryal, "The Self and Other People," *Journal of Philosophy: A Cross-Disciplinary Inquiry* 7, no. 16 (2011): 14–25, https://doi.org/10.5840/jphilnepal201171613.

84. Grégoire Chamayou and Janet Lloyd, *Drone Theory* (New York: Penguin, 2015), 14.

85. René Girard, *I See Satan Fall Like Lightning*, trans. James G. Williams (Maryknoll, NY: Orbis Books, 2001), 15.

86. Brian Urquhart, "Learning from Hammarskjöld," *New York Times*, September 16, 2011, http://www.nytimes.com/2011/09/17/opinion/learning-from-hammarskjold.html.

87. Costas M. Constantinou, "Human Diplomacy and Spirituality," *Clingendael Discussion Paper in Diplomacy* 103 (2006): 17, https://www.clingendael.org/publication/human-diplomacy-and-spirituality.

88. Elif Shafak, "Our Compass," *New York Times*, November 27, 2013, https://www.nytimes.com/2013/11/28/opinion/our-compass.html?pagewanted=3&_r=0.

89. Morgenthau, "The Evil of Politics and the Ethics of Evil," 13; Jodok Troy, "Desire for Power or the Power of Desire? Mimetic Theory and the Heart of Twentieth-Century Realism," *Journal of International Political Theory* 11, no. 1 (2015): 26–41.

90. J. S. Barkin, "Constructivism, Realism, and the Variety of Human Natures," in *Human Beings in International Relations*, ed. Daniel Jacobi and Annette Freyberg-Inan (Cambridge: Cambridge University Press, 2015), 165.

91. See, for example, Robert Powell, "Absolute and Relative Gains in International Relations Theory," *The American Political Science Review* 85, no. 4 (1991): 1303–20, https://doi.org/10.2307/1963947.

92. Jackson, *The Global Covenant*.

93. Alexander Wendt, "The State as Person in International Theory," *Review of International Studies* 30, no. 2 (2004): 289–316.

94. Lebow, *The Tragic Vision of Politics*.

95. Vassilios Paipais, "Between Politics and the Political: Reading Hans J. Morgenthau's Double Critique of Depoliticiastion," *Millennium: Journal of International Studies* 42, no. 2 (2014): 369.

Bibliography

Abdelal, Rawi, Yoshiko M. Herrera, Alastair Iain Johnston, and Rose McDermott. "Identity as a Variable." *Perspectives on Politics* 4, no. 4 (2006): 695–711.

Adams, Gordon, and Shoon Kathleen Murray, eds. *Mission Creep: The Militarization of US Foreign Policy?* Washington, DC: Georgetown University Press, 2014.

Agensky, Jonathan C. "Recognizing Religion: Politics, History, and the 'Long 19th Century.'" *European Journal of International Relations* 23 (2017): 729–55. doi: https://doi.org/10.1177/1354066116681428.

Ainley, Kirsten. "Excesses of Responsibility: The Limits of Law and the Possibilities of Politics." *Ethics & International Affairs* 25, no. 4 (2011): 407–31.

———. "Individual Agency and Responsibility for Atrocity." In *Confronting Evil in International Relations: Ethical Responses to Problems of Moral Agency*, edited by Renée Jeffery, 37–60. New York: Palgrave Macmillan, 2008.

———. "The Responsibility to Protect and the International Criminal Court: Counteracting the Crisis." *International Affairs* 91, no. 1 (2015): 37–54. doi: https://doi.org/10.1111/1468-2346.12185.

Allison, Graham T. *Essence of Decision: Explaining the Cuban Missile Crisis.* 2nd ed. Boston: Little, Brown, 1971.

Amin, Ash, and Nigel Thrift. *Seeing Like a City.* Cambridge, UK: Polity Press, 2016.

Amstutz, Mark R. "Restorative Justice, Political Forgiveness, and the Possibility of Political Reconciliation." In Philpott, *The Politics of Past Evil*, 151–88.

Angélil, Marc, and Cary Siress. "The Paris Banlieue: Peripheries of Inequity." *Journal of International Affairs* 65, no. 2 (2012): 57–67.

Antonello, Pierpaolo, and Paul Gifford, eds. *Can We Survive Our Origins? Readings in René Girard's Theory of Violence and the Sacred.* East Lansing: Michigan State University Press, 2015.

Appleby, Scott R. *The Ambivalence of the Sacred: Religion, Violence, and Reconciliation.* Lanham, MD: Rowman & Littlefield Publishers, 2000.

Arendt, Hannah. *Eichmann in Jerusalem: Ein Bericht von der Banalität des Bösen.* Munich: Piper, 2006.

———. *The Human Condition.* 2nd. ed. Chicago: University of Chicago Press, 2006.

Aron, Raymond. *In Defense of Political Reason: Essays.* Edited by Daniel J. Mahoney. Lanham, MD: Rowman & Littlefield, 1994.

———. *Frieden und Krieg: Eine Theorie der Staatenwelt.* Frankfurt am Main: S. Fischer, 1963.

Ashley, Richard K. "Political Realism and Human Interest." *International Studies Quarterly* 25 (1981): 204–36.

Ask, Sten, and Anna Mark-Jungkoist, eds. *The Adventure of Peace: Dag Hammarskjöld and the Future of the UN.* New York: Palgrave Macmillan, 2005.

Atran, Scott. *Talking to the Enemy: Violent Extremism, Sacred Values, and What It Means to Be Human.* London: Penguin, 2011.

Augustine. *Concerning the City of God Against the Pagans.* Translated by H. Bettension. London: Penguin Books, 2003.

Aulen, Gustav. *Dag Hammarskjöld's White Book: An Analysis of Markings.* London: SPCK, 1970.

Bailie, Gil. *Violence Unveiled: Humanity at the Crossroads.* New York: Crossroad Publishing Co., 1997.

Bain, William. *Between Anarchy and Society: Trusteeship and the Obligations of Power.* Oxford: Oxford University Press, 2004.

———. "Deconfusing Morgenthau: Moral Inquiry and Classical Realism Reconsidered." *Review of International Studies* 26, no. 3 (2000): 445–64.

Barber, Benjamin R. *Jihad vs. McWorld.* New York: Times Books, 1995.

Barkin, J. Samuel. "Constructivism, Realism, and the Variety of Human Natures." In *Human Beings in International Relations,* edited by Daniel Jacobi and Annette Freyberg-Inan, 156–71. Cambridge: Cambridge University Press, 2015.

———. *Realist Constructivism: Rethinking International Relations Theory.* Cambridge: Cambridge University Press, 2010.

Battilana, J. "Agency and Institutions: The Enabling Role of Individuals' Social Position." *Organization* 13, no. 5 (2006): 653–76.

Beall, J., T. Goodfellow, and D. Rodgers. "Cities and Conflict in Fragile States in the Developing World." *Urban Studies* 50, no. 15 (2013): 1–19. doi: https://doi.org/10.1177/0042098013487775.

Behr, Hartmut, and Amelia Heath. "Misreading in IR Theory and Ideology Critique: Morgenthau, Waltz and Neo-Realism." *Review of International Studies* 35 (2009): 327–49.

Bell, Duncan. "Political Realism and International Relations." *Philosophy Compass* 12, no. 2 (2017). doi: https://doi.org/10.1111/phc3.12403.

———. "What Is Liberalism?" *Political Theory* 42, no. 6 (2014): 682–715. doi: https://doi.org/10.1177/0090591714535103.

Berkowitz, Roger. "The Angry Jew Has Gotten His Revenge." *Philosophical Topics* 39, no. 2 (2011): 1–20. doi: https://doi.org/10.5840/philtopics20113921.

———. "The Power of Non-Reconciliation: Arendt's Judgment of Adolf Eichmann." *HannahArendt.net* 6, nos. 1/2 (2011). http://www.hannaharendt.net/index.php/han/article/view/11/8.

Bettiza, Gregorio, and Filippo Dionigi. "How Do Religious Norms Diffuse? Institutional Translation and International Change in a Post-Secular World Society." *European Journal of International Relations* 21, no. 3 (2015): 621–46.

Bevir, Mark, and R. A. W. Rhodes. "Interpretive Theory." In *Theory and Methods in Political Science*, 2nd ed., edited by David Marsh and Gerry Stoker, 131–52. New York: Palgrave Macmillan, 2002.

Bird, Kai, and Martin J. Sherwin. *American Prometheus: The Triumph and Tragedy of J. Robert Oppenheimer*. London: Atlantic, 2009.

Blok, Anton. "The Narcissism of Minor Differences." *European Journal of Social Theory* 1, no. 1 (1998): 33–56.

Bonhoeffer, Dietrich. *The Cost of Discipleship*. New York: Macmillan, 1963.

Booth, Ken, and Nicholas J. Wheeler. *The Security Dilemma: Fear, Cooperation, and Trust in World Politics*. London: Palgrave Macmillan, 2008.

Bourdieu, Pierre. *Distinction: A Social Critique of the Judgement of Taste*. Translated by Richard Nice. London: Routledge, 1984.

Brahm, Eric. "Uncovering the Truth: Examining Truth Commission Success and Impact." *International Studies Perspectives* 8, no. 1 (2007): 16–35. doi: https://doi.org/10.1111/j.1528-3585.2007.00267.x.

Brighi, Elisabetta. "The Globalisation of Resentment: Failure, Denial and Violence in World Politics." *Millennium: Journal of International Studies* 44, no. 3 (2016): 411–32.

Brighi, Elisabetta, and Antonio Cerella. "An Alternative Vision of Politics and Violence:

Introducing Mimetic Theory in International Studies." *Journal of International Political Theory* 11, no. 1 (2015): 3–25.

Brown, Chris. "The 'Practice Turn,' Phronesis and Classical Realism: Towards a Phronetic International Political Theory?" *Millennium: Journal of International Studies* 40, no. 3 (2012): 439–56.

Brown, Chris, and Robyn Eckersley, eds. *The Oxford Handbook of International Political Theory*. Oxford: Oxford University Press, 2018.

Bull, Hedley. *The Anarchical Society: A Study of Order in World Politics*. 4th ed. London: Palgrave Macmillan, 2012.

———. "International Theory: The Case for a Classical Approach." *World Politics* 18, no. 3 (1966): 361–77.

Burdett, Ricky. "Designing Urban Democracy: Mapping Scales of Urban Identity." *Public Culture* 25, no. 2 (2013): 349–67. doi: https://doi.org/10.1215/08992363-2020638.

Butterfield, Herbert. *Christianity, Diplomacy and War*. New York: Abingdon-Cokesbury Press, 1954.

———. *History and Human Relations*. London: HarperCollins, 1951.

Buzan, Barry. *From International to World Society? English School Theory and the Social Structure of Globalisation*. Cambridge: Cambridge University Press, 2004.

Byman, Daniel L., and Kenneth M. Pollack. "Let Us Now Praise Great Man: Bringing the Statesman Back In." *International Security* 25, no. 4 (2001): 107–46.

Cerella, Antonio. "Until the End of the World: Girard, Schmitt and the Origins of Violence." *Journal of International Political Theory* 11, no. 1 (2015): 42–60. doi: https://doi.org/10.1177/1755088214555457.

Chamayou, Grégoire. *Drone Theory*. Translated by Janet Lloyd. New York: Penguin, 2015.

Chesterton, Gilbert Keith. *Collected Works*. Vol. 1, *Heretics, Orthodoxy, The Blatchford Controversies* (San Francisco: Ignatius, 1986).

Chou, Mark. "Morgenthau, the Tragic: On Tragedy and the Transition from Scientific Man to Politics Among Nations." *Telos* 157 (2011): 109–28. doi: https://doi.org/10.3817/1211157109.

Constantinou, Costas M. "Human Diplomacy and Spirituality." *Clingendael Discussion Paper in Diplomacy* 103 (2006). https://www.clingendael.org/publication/human-diplomacy-and-spirituality.

Coward, Martin. "Network-Centric Violence, Critical Infrastructure and the Urbanization of Security." *Security Dialogue* 40, nos. 4–5 (2009): 399–418. doi: https://doi.org/10.1177/0967010609342879.

———. *Urbicide: The Politics of Urban Destruction*. London: Routledge, 2009.

Cowdell, Scott, Chris Fleming, and Joel Hodge, eds. *Violence, Desire, and the Sacred: Girard's Mimetic Theory Across the Disciplines*. New York: Continuum, 2012.

———, eds. *Violence, Desire, and the Sacred*, vol. 2, *René Girard and Sacrifice in Life, Love, and Literature*. London: Bloomsbury, 2014.

Cox, Robert W. "Social Forces, States and World Orders: Beyond International Relations Theory." *Millennium: Journal of International Studies* 10, no. 2 (1981): 126–55. doi: https://doi.org/10.1177/03058298810100020501.

Cozette, Murielle. "Realistic Realism? American Political Realism, Clausewitz and Raymond Aron on the Problem of Means and Ends in International Politics." *Journal of Strategic Studies* 27, no. 3 (2004): 428–53.

———. "What Lies Ahead: Classical Realism on the Future of International Relations." *International Studies Review* 10 (2008): 667–79.

Craig, Campbell. *Glimmer of a New Leviathan: Total War in the Realism of Niebuhr, Morgenthau, and Waltz*. New York: Columbia University Press, 2007.

Cruise O'Brien, Connor. "Common Sense and Unjust Wars." In *Religion and International Affairs*, edited by Jeffrey Rose and Michael Ignatieff, 20–25. Toronto: Anansi, 1968.

Dacey, Austin. *The Secular Conscience: Why Belief Belongs in Public Life*. Amherst, NY: Prometheus Books, 2008.

Dallmayr, Fred. "A Global Spiritual Resurgence? On Christian and Islamic Spiritualities." In *Religion in International Relations: The Return from Exile*, edited by Pavlos a. P. F. Hatzopoulos, 209–36. New York: Palgrave Macmillan, 2003.

Davies, James C. "Towards a Theory of Revolution." *American Sociological Review* 27, no. 1 (1962): 5–19.

Davis, Mike. *Planet of Slums*. New York: Verso, 2006.

Deaton, Clifford. "The Revolution Will Not Be Occupied: Theorizing Urban Revolutionary Movements in Tehran, Prague, and Paris." *Territory, Politics, Governance* 3, no. 2 (2015): 205–26. doi: https://doi.org/10.1080/21622671.2014.945473.

Desh, Michael C. "America's Liberal Illiberalism: The Ideological Origins of Overreaction in U.S. Foreign Policy." *International Security* 32, no. 3 (2007/2008): 7–43.

Dike, Mustafa. "Disruptive Politics." *Urban Studies* 54, no. 1 (2017): 49–54. doi: https://doi.org/10.1177/0042098016671476.

Dikec, Mustafa. *Urban Rage: The Revolt of the Excluded*. New Haven, CT: Yale University Press, 2018.

Dionigi, Filippo. "Dag Hammarskjöld's Religiosity and Norms Entrepreneurship: A Post-Secular Perspective." *Politics and Religion* 9, no. 1 (2016): 162–86.

Durkheim, Émile. *The Elementary Forms of the Religious Life*. Translated by Joseph Ward Swain. Mineola, NY: Dover Publications Inc., 2008. .

Edkins, Jenny, and Maja Zehfuss. "Generalising the International." *Review of International Studies* 31, no. 3 (2005): 451–71.

Eliade, Mircea. *The Sacred and the Profane: The Nature of Religion*. Translated by Willard R. Trask. San Diego: Harcourt, 1987.

Enzensberger, Hans Magnus. *Aussichten auf den Bürgerkrieg*. Frankfurt: Suhrkamp, 1993.

———. *Civil War*. London: Granta Books, 1994.

"""Etzioni, Amitai. "The Democratisation Mirage." *Survival* 57, no. 4 (2015): 139–56. doi: https://doi.org/10.1080/00396338.2015.1068570.

Fanon, Frantz, and Richard Philcox. *The Wretched of the Earth*. New York: Grove Press, 2004.

Farneti, Roberto. "Bipolarity Redux: The Mimetic Context of the 'New Wars.'" *Cambridge Review of International Affairs* 26, no. 1 (2013): 181–202. doi: https://doi.org/10.108 0/09557571.2012.737305.

———. "A Mimetic Perspective on Conflict Resolution." *Polity* 41, no. 4 (2009): 536–58. doi: https://doi.org/10.1057/pol.2009.2.

———. *Mimetic Politics: Dyadic Patterns in Global Politics*. East Lansing: Michigan State University Press, 2015.

Favazza, Joseph A. "Reconciliation: On the Border Between Theological and Political Praxis." *Journal for the Study of Religions and Ideologies* 1, no. 6 (2002): 52–64.

Finlayson, L. "With Radicals Like These, Who Needs Conservatives? Doom, Gloom, and Realism in Political Theory." *European Journal of Political Theory* 16, no. 3 (2017): 264–82.

Finnemore, Martha. "Exporting the English School?" *Review of International Studies* 27 (2001): 509–13.

———. *National Interests in International Society*. Ithaca, NY: Cornell University Press, 1996.

Fisk, Kerstin, and Jennifer M. Ramos. "Actions Speak Louder Than Words: Preventive Self-Defense as a Cascading Norm." *International Studies Perspectives* 15, no. 2 (2013): 163–85. doi: https://doi.org/10.1111/insp.12013.

Foote, Wilder, ed. *Dag Hammarskjöld: Servant of Peace; A Selection of His Speeches and Statements*. New York: Harper & Row, 1962.

Frank, Robert H. *Choosing the Right Pond: Human Behavior and the Quest for Status*. Oxford: Oxford University Press, 1986.

Frankl, Victor E. *Man's Search for Meaning*. London: Rider, 2004.

Fraser, Giles. *Christianity and Violence: Girard, Nietzsche, Anselm and Tutu*. London: Darton, Longman and Todd, 2001.

Frei, Christoph. *Hans J. Morgenthau: Eine intellektuelle Biographie*. Bern: Haupt, 1993.

Freud, Sigmund, James Strachey, and Albert Dickson. *Civilization, Society and Religion: Group Psychology, Civilization and Its Discontents and Other Works*. London: Penguin Books, 1991.

Friedman, Thomas L. *The World Is Flat: The Globalized World in the Twenty-First Century*. London: Penguin Books, 2006.

Friedrichs, Jörg, and Friedrich Kratochwil. "On Acting and Knowing: How Pragmatism Can Advance International Relations Research and Methodology." *International Organization* 63, no. 4 (2009): 701–31. doi: https://doi.org/10.1017/ S0020818309990142.

Friis, Simone Molin. "'Behead, Burn, Crucify, Crush': Theorizing the Islamic State's Public Displays of Violence." *European Journal of International Relations* 24 (2017): 243–67.

———. "'Beyond Anything We Have Ever Seen': Beheading Videos and the Visibility of Violence in the War Against ISIS." *International Affairs* 91 (2015): 725–46. https:// doi.org/10.1111/1468-2346.12341.

Fröhlich, Manuel. *Dag Hammarskjöld und die Vereinten Nationen: Die politische Ethik des Generalsekretärs*. Paderborn: Schöning, 2002.

———. *Political Ethics and the United Nations: Dag Hammarskjöld as Secretary-General*. New York: Routledge, 2008.

Frost, Mervyn, and Silviya Lechner. "Two Conceptions of International Practice: Aristotelian Praxis or Wittgensteinian Language-Games?" *Review of International Studies* 42, no. 2 (2016): 334–50. doi: https://doi.org/10.1177/1755088215596765.

———. "Understanding International Practices from the Internal Point of View." *Journal of International Political Theory* 12, no. 3 (2016): 299–319. doi: https://doi. org/10.1177/1755088215596765.

Frost, Mervyn. "Constitutive Theory and Moral Accountability: Individuals, Institutions, and Disperse Practices." In *Can Institutions Have Responsibilities? Collective Moral Agency and International Relations*, edited by Toni Erskine, 84–99. Houndmills, NY: Palgrave Macmillan, 2003.

Fuchs, Barbara. *Mimesis and Empire: The New World, Islam, and European Identities*. Cambridge: Cambridge University Press, 2001.

Fukuyama, Francis. *Identity: The Demand for Dignity and the Politics of Resentment*. New York: Farrar Straus and Giroux, 2018.

———. *Political Order and Political Decay: From the Industrial Revolution to the Globalization of Democracy*. London: Farrar Straus and Giroux, 2014.

Galtung, Johan. *Strukturelle Gewalt: Beiträge zur Friedens- und Konfliktforschung*. Reinbek bei Hamburg: Rowohlt, 1975.

Gardner, Stephen L. "Rene Girard's Apocalyptic Critique of Historical Reason: Limiting Politics to Make Way for Faith." *Contagion: Journal of Violence, Mimesis, and Culture* 18 (2011): 1–22.

Geertz, Clifford. *Local Knowledge: Further Essays in Interpretative Anthropology*. New York: Basic Books, 1983.

———. "Thick Description: Toward an Interpretative Theory of Culture." In *The Interpretation of Cultures*, edited by Clifford Geertz, 3–30. New York: Basic Books, 1973.

Germes, Mélina, and Georg Glasze. "Die Banlieus als Gegenorte der République: Eine Diskursanalyse neuer Sicherheitspolitiken in den Vorstädten Frankreichs." *Geographica Helvetica* 65, no. 3 (2010): 217–28.

Gilpin, Robert. *The Political Economy of International Relations*. Princeton, NJ: Princeton University Press, 1987.

Girard, René. *Das Ende der Gewalt: Analyse des Menschheitsverhängnisses*. Freiburg im Breisgau: Herder, 1983.

———. *Das Heilige und die Gewalt*. Düsseldorf: Patmos, 2006.

———. *Deceit, Desire, and the Novel: Self and Other in Literary Structure*. Baltimore: Johns Hopkins University Press, 1976.

———. *Evolution and Conversion: Dialogues on the Origin of Culture*. With Pierpaolo Antonello and Joao Cezar de Castro Rocha. London: Continuum, 2008.

———. *Figuren des Begehrens: Das Selbst und der Andere in der fiktionalen Realität*. Wien: LIT, 1999.

———. *I See Satan Fall Like Lightning*. Translated by James G. Williams. Maryknoll, NY: Orbis Books, 2001.

———. *Ich sah den Satan vom Himmel fallen wie einen Blitz: Eine kritische Apologie des Christentums*. Munich: Hanser, 2002.

———. "On War and Apocalypse." *First Things*, August/September 2009, 17–22.

———. *The One by Whom Scandal Comes*. East Lansing: Michigan State University Press, 2014.

———. *The Scapegoat*. Baltimore: Johns Hopkins University Press, 1986.

———. *A Theater of Envy: William Shakespeare*. Oxford: Oxford University Press, 1991.

———. *Things Hidden Since the Foundation of the World: Research Undertaken in Collaboration with Jean-Michel Oughourlian and Guy Lefort*. Translated by Michael Metteer (book 1) and Stephen Bann (books 2 & 3). London: Athlone Press, 1987.

———. "Triangular Desire." In *The Girard Reader*, edited by René Girard and James G. Williams, 33–44. New York: Crossroad and Herder, 1996.

———. *Violence and the Sacred*. Baltimore: Johns Hopkins University Press, 1979.

Girard, René, and Benoît Chantre. *Battling to the End: Conversations with Benoît Chantre*. East Lansing: Michigan State University Press, 2010.

———. *Im Angesicht der Apokalypse: Clausewitz zu Ende Denken; Gespräche mit Benoît Chantre*. Berlin: Matthes et Seitz Berlin, 2014.

Girard, René, and Wolfgang Palaver. *Gewalt Und Religion, Ursache Oder Wirkung?* Berlin: Matthes & Seitz, 2010.

Girard, René, and Henri Tincq. "What Is Happening Today Is Mimetic Rivalry on a Global Scale." *South Central Revue* 19, nos. 2/3 (2002): 22–27.

Gismondi, Mark. "Tragedy, Realism, and Postmodernity: Kulturpessimismus in the Theories of Max Weber, E. H. Carr, Hans J. Morgenthau, and Henry Kissinger." *Diplomacy & Statecraft* 15, no. 3 (2004): 435–64.

Gladwyn, Jebb. *The Memoirs of Lord Gladwyn*. New York: Weybright Talley, 1972.

Goldstein, Joshua S. *Winning the War on War: The Decline of Armed Conflict Worldwide*. New York: Dutton, 2011.

Goldstein, Judith, and Robert O. Keohane, eds. *Ideas and Foreign Policy: Beliefs, Institutions, and Political Change*. Ithaca, NY: Cornell University Press, 1993.

Goodhart, Sandor, and Yubraj Aryal. "The Self and Other People." *Journal of Philosophy: A Cross-Disciplinary Inquiry* 7, no. 16 (2011): 14–25. doi: https://doi.org/10.5840/jphilnepal201171613.

Green, Daniel M. "Introduction to the English School in International Studies." In Navari and Green, *Guide to the English School in International Studies*, 1–6.

Greenblum, Jake. "Distributive and Retributive Desert in Rawls." *Journal of Social Philosophy* 41, no. 2 (2010): 169–84. doi: https://doi.org/10.1111/j.1467-9833.2010.01485.x.

Gruenler, Curtis. "C. S. Lewis and René Girard on Desire, Conversion, and Myth: The Case of 'till We Have Faces.'" *Christianity & Literature* 60, no. 2 (2011): 247–65.

Grzymala-Busse, Anna. "The Difficulty with Doctrine: How Religion Can Influence Politics." *Government and Opposition* 51 (2016): 327–50. doi: https://doi.org/10.1017/gov.2015.38.

Guggenberger, Wilhelm, and Wolfgang Palaver, eds. *Eskalation zum Aussersten? Girards Clausewitz interdisziplinar kommentiert*. Baden-Baden: Nomos Verlagsgesellschaft, 2015.

Guilhot, Nicolas. *After the Enlightenment: Political Realism and International Relations in the Mid-Twentieth Century*. Cambridge: Cambridge University Press, 2017.

———. "American Katechon: When Political Theology Became International Relations Theory." *Constellations* 17, no. 2 (2010): 224–53.

———, ed. *The Invention of International Relations Theory: Realism, the Rockefeller Foundation, and the 1954 Conference on Theory*. New York: Columbia University Press, 2011.

Gunning, Jeroen, and Richard Jackson. "What's So 'Religious' about 'Religious Terrorism'?"

Critical Studies on Terrorism 4 (2011): 369–88. doi: https://doi.org/10.1080/175391 53.2011.623405.

Gurr, Ted Robert. *Why Men Rebel*. Princeton, NJ: Princeton University Press, 1970.

Habermas, Jürgen. *Glauben und Wissen*. Frankfurt: Suhrkamp, 2001.

Habermas, Jürgen, and Joseph Ratzinger. *Dialektik der Säkularisierung: Über Vernunft und Religion*. 7th ed. Freiburg: Herder, 2005.

Hall, Christopher A. "Truth, Pluralism, and Religious Diplomacy: A Christian Dialogical Perspective." In *Religion & Security: The New Nexus in International Relations*. Edited by Robert A. Seiple and Dennis R. Hoover, 83–97. Oxford: Rowman & Littlefield Publishers, 2004.

Hamerton-Kelly, Robert, ed. *Violent Origins: Walter Burkert, René Girard & Jonathan Z. Smith on Ritual Killing and Cultural Formation*. Stanford, CA: Stanford University Press, 1987.

Hammar, K. G. "Dag Hammarskjöld and Markings." In Ask and Mark-Jungkoist, *The Adventure of Peace*, 110–25.

Hammarskjöld, Dag. *Markings*. Translated by Leif Sjöberg and W. H. Auden. New York: Vintage Spiritual Classics, 2006.

Hanley, Ryan Patrick. "Political Science and Political Understanding: Isaiah Berlin on the Nature of Political Inquiry." *American Political Science Review* 98, no. 2 (2004): 327–39. doi: https://doi.org/10.1017/S0003055404001170.

Hardy, Richard P. "Hammarskjöld, the Mystic." *Ephemerides Carmeliticae* 29 (1978): 266–77.

Hartz, Louis. *The Liberal Tradition in America: An Interpretation of American Political Thought Since the Revolution*. New York: Harcourt Brace Jovanovich, 1955.

Hasan, A. "Can Urban Density Be Made to Work for Everyone? Exploring Options for Karachi's Low- and Lower-Middle-Class Settlements." *Environment and Urbanization* 22, no. 1 (2010): 267–68. doi: https://doi.org/10.1177/0956247810364116.

Herborth, Benjamin. "Imagining Man—Forgetting Society?" In Jacobi and Freyberg-Inan, *Human beings in international relations*, 229–46.

Hobbes, Thomas. *The Leviathan*. Cambridge: Cambridge University Press, 1991.

Hollis, Martin, and Steve Smith. *Explaining and Understanding International Relations*. Oxford: Oxford University Press, 1990.

Hondrich, Karl Otto. *Wieder Krieg*. Frankfurt: Suhrkamp, 2002.

Honig, Bonnie. *Political Theory and the Displacement of Politics*. Ithaca, NY: Cornell University Press, 1993.

Howard, Michael. *The Invention of Peace: Reflections on War and International Order*. New Haven, CT: Yale University Press, 2001.

Huntington, Samuel P. *The Clash of Civilizations and the Remaking of World Order*. New York: Simon & Schuster, 2003.

———. *The Third Wave: Democratization in the Late Twentieth Century*. Norman: University of Oklahoma Press, 1993.

Hurd, Elizabeth Shakman. *The Politics of Secularism in International Relations*. Princeton, NJ: Princeton University Press, 2008.

Hurd, Ian. "'If I Had a Rocket Launcher': Self-Defense and Forever War in International Law." *Houston Law Review* 56, no. 4 (2019): 821–39.

Hutchison, Emma, and Roland Bleiker. "Theorizing Emotions in World Politics." *International Theory* 6, no. 3 (2014): 491–514. doi: https://doi.org/10.1017/S175297191400023.

Isaak, Robert A. *Individuals and World Politics*. North Scituate, MA: Duxbury Press, 1975.

Ish-Shalom, Piki. "The Triptych of Realism, Elitism, and Conservatism." *International Studies Review* 8 (2006): 441–68.

Jackson, Patrick Thaddeus. *The Conduct of Inquiry in International Relations*. London: Routledge, 2009.

Jackson, Patrick T., and D. H. Nexon. "Relations Before States: Substance, Process and the Study of World Politics." *European Journal of International Relations* 5, no. 3 (1999): 291–332.

Jackson, Robert. *The Global Covenant: Human Conduct in a World of States*. New York: Oxford University Press, 2000.

Jacobi, Daniel, and Annette Freyberg-Inan, eds. *Human Beings in International Relations*. Cambridge: Cambridge University Press, 2015.

Jacoby, T. A. "A Theory of Victimhood: Politics, Conflict and the Construction of Victim-Based Identity." *Millennium: Journal of International Studies* 43, no. 2 (2015): 511–30.

Jervis, Robert. "Hans Morgenthau, Realism, and the Scientific Study of International Politics." *Social Research* 61, no. 4 (1994): 853–76.

———. *Perception and Misperception in International Politics*. Princeton, NJ: Princeton University Press, 1976.

Johnsen, William A. "Geoffrey Hill, René Girard, and the Logic of Sacrifice." *Religion and the Arts* 16, no. 5 (2012): 573–80. doi: https://doi.org/10.1163/15685292-12341240.

Johnson, Edward. "The British and the 1960 Soviet Attack on the Office of United Nations Secretary-General." *Diplomacy & Statecraft* 14, no. 1 (2003): 79–102.

Johnston, Ysabel. "Mimesis and Ritual: Girardian Critique of the Social Contract." *Res Cogitans* 5, no. 1 (2014): 169–77.

Jones, Dorothy V. "The Example of Dag Hammarskjöld: Style and Effectiveness at the UN." *Christian Century* 111, no. 32 (1994): 1047–50.

———. "Seeking Balance: The Secretary-General as Normative Negotiator." In Kille, *The UN Secretary-General and Moral Authority*, 39–66.

———. "The World Outlook of Dag Hammarskjöld." In *Ethics and Statecraft: The Moral Dimension of International Affairs*, 2nd ed., edited by Cathal J. Nolan, 133–46. Westport, CT: Praeger, 2004.

Jönsson, Christer, and Martin Hall. *Essence of Diplomacy*. London: Palgrave Macmillan, 2005.

Juergensmeyer, Mark. *Global Rebellion: Religious Challenges to the Secular State from Christian Militias to Al Qaeda*. Berkeley: University of California Press, 2008.

———. *The New Cold War? Religious Nationalism Confronts the Secular State*. Berkeley: University of California Press, 1994.

Jütersonke, O., R. Muggah, and D. Rodgers. "Gangs, Urban Violence, and Security Interventions in Central America." *Security Dialogue* 40, nos. 4–5 (2009): 373–97. doi: https://doi.org/10.1177/0967010609343298.

Kahn, Paul W. *Sacred Violence: Torture, Terror, and Sovereignty*. Ann Arbor: University of Michigan Press, 2008.

Kantorowicz, Ernst. *The King's Two Bodies: A Study in Mediaeval Political Theology*. 7th ed. Princeton, NJ: Princeton University Press, 1997.

Kaplan, Robert D. *Balkan Ghosts: A Journey Through History*. New York: Picador; Distributed by Holtzbrinck Publishers, 2005.

———. *The Coming Anarchy: Shattering the Dreams of the Post Cold War*. New York: Vintage Books, 2001.

———. *The Ends of the Earth: From Togo to Turkmenistan, from Iran to Cambodia; A Journey to the Frontiers of Anarchy*. New York: Vintage Books, 1997.

———. *Warrior Politics: Why Leadership Demands a Pagan Ethos*. New York: Random House, 2002.

Keohane, Robert O. "Big Questions in the Study of World Politics." In *The Oxford Handbook of International Relations*, edited by Christian Reus-Smit and Duncan Snidal, 708–15. Oxford: Oxford University Press, 2010.

Khanna, Parag. *The Second World: How Emerging Powers Are Redefining Global Competition in the Twenty-First Century*. London: Penguin Books, 2008.

Khoury, Nadim. "Political Reconciliation: With or Without Grand Narratives?" *Constellations* 24, no. 2 (2017): 245–56. doi: https://doi.org/10.1111/1467-8675.12237.

Kille, Kent J., ed. *The UN Secretary-General and Moral Authority: Ethics and Religion in International Leadership*. Washington, DC: Georgetown University Press, 2007.

Kirshner, Jonathan. "The Economic Sins of Modern IR Theory and the Classical Realist

Alternative." *World Politics* 67, no. 1 (2014): 155–83. doi: https://doi.org/10.1017/ S0043887114000318.

Kissinger, Henry. *World Order: Reflections on the Character of Nations and the Course of History*. London: Alan Lane, 2014.

Kohen, Ari, Michael Zanchelli, and Levi Drake. "Personal and Political Reconciliation in Post-Genocide Rwanda." *Social Justice Research* 24, no. 1 (2011): 85–106.

Koskenniemi, Martti. *The Gentle Civilizer of Nations: The Rise and Fall of International Law, 1870–1960*. Cambridge: Cambridge University Press, 2002.

Kratochwil, Friedrich. *Praxis: On Acting and Knowing*. Cambridge: Cambridge University Press, 2018.

Krause, Jill, and Neil Renwick, eds. *Identities in International Relations*. Basingstoke: St. Martin's Press, 1996.

Lang, Anthony F. "Morgenthau, Agency, and Aristotle." In Williams, *Realism Reconsidered*, 18–41.

———, ed. *Political Theory and International Affairs: Hans J. Morgenthau on Aristotle's 'the Politics.'* Westport, CT: Praeger, 2004.

Lash, Joseph P. *Dag Hammarskjöld: Custodian of the Bushfire Peace*. Garden City, NY: Doubleday, 1961.

Laurent, Paul, and Gilles Paquet. "Intercultural Relations: A Myrdal—Tocqueville—Girard Interpretive Scheme." *International Political Science Review* 12, no. 3 (1991): 171–83.

Lebow, Richard Ned. "Identity and International Relations." *International Relations* 22, no. 4 (2008): 473–92.

———. *The Tragic Vision of Politics: Ethics, Interests and Orders*. Cambridge: Cambridge University Press, 2003.

Levy, Jack S. "International Sources for Interstate and Intrastate War." In *Leashing the Dogs of War: Conflict Management in a Divided World*. Edited by Chester A. Crocker, 17–38. Washington, DC: United States Institute of Peace Press, 2008.

Linfield, Susie. "Trading Truth for Justice? Reflections on South Africa's Truth and Reconciliation Commission." *Boston Review*, 2000, http://new.bostonreview.net/ BR25.3/linfield.html.

Linklater, Andrew, and Hidemi Suganami. *The English School of International Relations: A Contemporary Reassessment*. Cambridge: Cambridge University Press, 2006.

Liotta, P. H., and James F. Miskel. "The 'Mega-Eights': Urban Leviathans and International Instability." *Orbis* 53, no. 4 (2009): 647–63. doi: https://doi.org/10.1016/j. orbis.2009.07.003.

Lipsey, Roger. *Hammarskjöld: A Life*. Ann Arbor: University of Michigan Press, 2013.

Lobell, Steven E., Norrin M. Ripsman, and Jeffrey W. Taliaferro, eds. *Neoclassical Realism, the State, and Foreign Policy*. Cambridge: Cambridge University Press, 2009.

Marin, Lou. "Can We Save True Dialogue in an Age of Mistrust? The Encounter of Dag Hammarskjöld and Martin Buber." *Critical Currents* 8 (2010).

Lynch, Cecelia. *Interpreting International Politics*. New York: Routledge, 2014.

———. "A Neo-Weberian Approach to Religion in International Politics." *International Theory* 1, no. 3 (2009): 381–408.

Lyon, Alynna J. "The UN Charter, the New Testament, and the Psalms: The Moral Authority of Dag Hammarskjöld." In Kille, *The UN Secretary-General and Moral Authority*, 111–41.

MacIntyre, Alasdair. *After Virtue: A Study in Moral Theory*. Notre Dame, IN: University of Notre Dame Press, 1981.

Marc, Alexandre, and Alys M. Willman. *Violence in the City: Understanding and Supporting Community Responses to Urban Violence*. Washington, DC: World Bank, 2010.

Marcuse, Peter. "The 'War on Terrorism' and Life in Cities after September 11, 2001." In *Cities, War, and Terrorism: Towards an Urban Geopolitics*, edited by Stephen Graham, 263–75. Malden, MA: Blackwell Publishing, 2004.

Marr, Andrew. *Tools for Peace: The Spiritual Craft of St. Benedict and René Girard*. New York: iUniverse, 2007.

Mattern, Janice Bially. "On Being Convinced: An Emotional Epistemology of International Relations." *International Theory* 6, no. 3 (2014): 589–94. doi: https://doi.org/10.1017/S1752971914000323.

May, Samantha, Erin K. Wilson, Claudia Baumgart-Ochse, and Faiz Sheikh. "The Religious as Political and the Political as Religious: Globalisation, Post-Secularism and the Shifting Boundaries of the Sacred." *Politics, Religion & Ideology* 15, no. 3 (2014): 331–46.

Mayall, James. "Introduction." In *The Diplomatic Corps as an Institution of International Society*, edited by Paul Sharp and Geoffrey Wiseman, 1–12. London: Palgrave Macmillan, 2007.

Mazrui, Ali A. *Cultural Forces in World Politics*. Oxford: J. Currey, 2000.

McCourt, David M. "Practice Theory and Relationalism as the New Constructivism." *International Studies Quarterly* 60, no. 3 (2016): 475–85.

McFarlane, Colin. "The Geographies of Urban Density." *Progress in Human Geography* 40, no. 5 (2016): 629–48. doi: https://doi.org/10.1177/0309132515608694.

McGinn, Bernard. *The Foundations of Christian Mysticism: The Presence of God; A History of Western Christian Mysticism*. New York: Crossroad, 1991.

McQueen, Alison. "The Case for Kinship: Classical Realism and Political Realism." In

Politics Recovered: Realist Thought in Theory and Practice, edited by Matt Sleat. New York: Columbia University Press, 2018.

———. "Political Realism and Moral Corruption." *European Journal of Political Theory* (2016): 1–21.

———. "Political Realism and the Realist 'Tradition.'" *Critical Review of International Social and Political Philosophy* 20, no. 3 (2017): 296–313. doi: https://doi.org/10.1080 /13698230.2017.1293914.

Mearsheimer, John J. *The Great Delusion: Liberal Dreams and International Realities.* New Haven, CT: Yale University Press, 2018.

———. "Why the Ukraine Crisis Is the West's Fault." *Foreign Affairs* 93, no. 5 (2014): 1–12.

Micklethwait, John, and Adrian Wooldridge. *God Is Back: How the Global Revival of Faith Is Challenging the World.* London: Penguin Books, 2009.

Mihai, Mihaela. "When the State Says 'Sorry': State Apologies as Exemplary Political Judgments." *Journal of Political Philosophy* 21, no. 2 (2013): 200–220. doi: https://doi. org/10.1111/j.1467-9760.2012.00418.x.

Mihelj, Sabina. "'Faith in Nation Comes in Different Guises': Modernist Versions of Religious Nationalism." *Nations and Nationalism* 13, no. 2 (2007): 265–84.

Mishra, Pankaj. *Age of Anger: A History of the Present.* New York: Penguin, 2018.

Mollov, Ben. *Power and Transcendence: Hans J. Morgenthau and the Jewish Experience.* Lanham, MD: Lexington, 2002.

Mollov, Ben, Ephraim Meir, and Chaim Lavie. "An Integrated Strategy for Peacebuilding: Judaic Approaches." *Die Friedenswarte: Journal of International Peace and Organization* 82, no. 2–3 (2007): 137–58.

Molloy, Seán. "Truth, Power, Theory: Hans Morgenthau's Formulation of Realism." *Diplomacy & Statecraft* 15, no. 1 (2004): 1–34. doi: https://doi. org/10.1080/09592290490438042.

Morgenthau, Hans J. "Does Disarmament Mean Peace?" In *Arms and Foreign Policy in the Nuclear Age*, edited by Milton J. Rakokove, 417–23. New York: Oxford University Press, 1972.

———. "The Evil of Politics and the Ethics of Evil." *Ethics* 56, no. 1 (1945): 1–18.

———. "An Intellectual Autobiography." *Society in Transition* 15 (1978): 63–68.

———. *Politics Among Nations: The Struggle for Power and Peace.* New York: Knopf, 1948.

———. *Politics Among Nations: The Struggle for Power and Peace.* 5th ed. New York: A. A. Knopf, 1973.

———. *Politics in the Twentieth Century.* Chicago: University of Chicago Press, 1971.

———. "Positivism, Functionalism, and International Law." *American Journal of International Law* 34, no. 2 (1940): 260–84.

———. *Science: Servant or Master?* New York: New American Library, 1972.

———. "Science of Peace: A Rationalist Utopia." *Social Research* 42, no. 1 (1975): 20–34.

———. *Scientific Man vs. Power Politics.* Chicago: University of Chicago Press, 1946.

———. "The Twilight of International Morality." *Ethics* 58, no. 2 (1948): 79–99.

Morgenthau, Hans J., Hartmut Behr, and Felix Rösch. *The Concept of the Political.* New York: Palgrave Macmillan, 2012.

Morton, Adam. *On Evil.* New York: Routledge, 2004.

Mouffe, Chantal. *On the Political.* London: Routledge, 2006.

Muggah, Robert. *Researching the Urban Dilemma: Urbanization, Poverty and Violence.* Ottawa: International Development Research Centre, 2012.

Murray, A. J. H. "The Moral Politics of Hans Morgenthau." *Review of Politics* 58, no. 1 (1996): 81–107.

Nagel, Thomas. *The View from Nowhere.* Oxford: Oxford University Press, 1989.

Navari, Cornelia. "The Concept of Practice in the English School." *European Journal of International Relations* 17, no. 4 (2011): 611–30.

———. "English School Methodology." In Navari and Green, *Guide to the English School in International Studies*, 205–21.

———. "Introduction: Methods and Methodology in the English School." In *Theorising International Society: English School Methods*, edited by Cornelia Navari, 1–20. London: Palgrave Macmillan, 2009.

Navari, Cornelia, and Daniel M. Green, eds. *Guide to the English School in International Studies.* West Sussex: Wiley-Blackwell, 2014.

Nayar, Kaladharan M. G. "Dag Hammarskjöld and U Thant: The Evolution of Their Offices." *Case Western Reserve Journal of International Law* 36 (1974): 36–83.

Nelson, Joan. "The Urban Poor: Disruption or Political Integration in Third World Cities?" *World Politics* 22, no. 3 (1970): 393–414.

Neufled Redekop, Vern, and Thomas Ryba, eds. *René Girard and Creative Reconciliation.* Lanham, MD: Lexington Books, 2014.

Neumann, Franz L. "Approaches of the Study of Power." *Political Science Quarterly*, 65, no. 2 (1950): 161–80.

Neumann, Iver B. "Self and Other in International Relations." *European Journal of International Relations* 2, no. 2 (1996): 139–74.

Nishimura, Kuniyuki. "E. H. Carr, Dostoevsky, and the Problem of Irrationality in Modern Europe." *International Relations* 25, no. 1 (2011): 45–64.

Nunan, Timothy. *Humanitarian Invasion: Global Development in Cold War Afghanistan.* Cambridge: Cambridge University Press, 2016.

Bibliography 125

Oakeshott, Michael. *On Human Conduct.* Oxford: Clarendon Press, 1975.

O'Brien, Conor Cruise. *To Katanga and Back.* New York: Simon & Schuster, 1962.

Oren, Ido. *Our Enemies and US: America's Rivalries and the Making of Political Science.* Ithaca, NY: Cornell University Press, 2003.

———. "The Unrealism of Contemporary Realism: The Tension Between Realist Theory and Realists' Practice." *Perspectives on Politics* 7, no. 2 (2009): 283–301.

Paipais, Vassilios. "Between Politics and the Political: Reading Hans J. Morgenthau's Double Critique of Depoliticisation." *Millennium: Journal of International Studies* 42, no. 2 (2014): 354–75.

———. "Introduction: Political Theologies of the International—the Continued Relevance of Theology in International Relations." *Journal of International Relations and Development* 22, no. 2 (2019): 269–77. doi: https://doi.org/10.1057/s41268-018-0160-2.

———. "Necessary Fiction: Realism's Tragic Theology." *International Politics* 50, no. 6 (2013): 846–62. doi: https://doi.org/10.1057/ip.2013.38.

Palaver, Wolfgang. "Envy or Emulation: A Christian Understanding of Economic Passions." In *Passions in Economy, Politics, and the Media: In Discussion with Christian Theology*, edited by Wolfgang Palaver and Petra Steinmair-Pösel, 139–62. Münster: LIT, 2005.

———. "René Girard's Contribution to Political Theology: Overcoming Deadlocks of Competition and Enmity." In *Between Philosophy and Theology: Contemporary Interpretations of Christianity*, edited by L. Boeve and Christophe Brabant, 149–65. Burlington, VT: Ashgate Pub., 2010.

———. *René Girard's Mimetic Theory.* East Lansing: Michigan State University Press, 2013.

Parent, Joseph M., and Joshua M. Baron. "Elder Abuse: How the Moderns Mistreat Classical Realism." *International Studies Review* 13 (2011): 193–213.

Pearse, Meic. *Why the Rest Hates the West: Understanding the Roots of Global Rage.* Downers Grove, IL: InterVarsity Press, 2004.

Philpott, Daniel. "Beyond Politics as Usual: Is Reconciliations Compatible with Liberalism?" In Philpott, *The Politics of Past Evil*, 11–44.

———. "Iraq's Urgent Need for a Reconciliation Ethic." *America*, April 4, 2005, http://americamagazine.org/issue/526/article/iraqs-urgent-need-reconciliation-ethic.

———. *Just and Unjust Peace: An Ethic of Political Reconciliation.* New York: Oxford University Press, 2012.

———. "The Justice of Forgiveness." *Journal of Religious Ethics* 41, no. 3 (2013): 400–416. doi: https://doi.org/10.1111/jore.12021.

———, ed. *The Politics of Past Evil: Religion, Reconciliation, and the Dilemmas of Transitional Justice.* Notre Dame, IN: University of Notre Dame Press, 2006.

Plato. *The Republic*. Edited by G. R. F. Ferraris. Translated by T. Griffith. Cambridge: Cambridge University Press, 2000.

Polat, Necati. *International Relations, Meaning and Mimesis*. New York: Routledge, 2012.

Powell, Robert. "Absolute and Relative Gains in International Relations Theory." *American Political Science Review* 85, no. 4 (1991): 1303–20. doi: https://doi. org/10.2307/1963947.

Raleigh, Clionadh. "Urban Violence Patterns Across African States." *International Studies Review* 17, no. 1 (2015): 90–106. doi: https://doi.org/10.1111/misr.12206.

Rawls, John. *Political Liberalism*. New York: Columbia University Press, 2005.

——. *A Theory of Justice*. Cambridge, MA: Belknap Press, 2005.

Reiss, Mitchell. *Bridled Ambition: Why Countries Constrain Their Nuclear Capabilities*. Washington, DC: Woodrow Wilson Center Press, 1995.

Rengger, Nicholas. "Political Theory and International Relations: Promised Land or Exit from Eden?" *International Affairs* 76, no. 4 (2000): 755–70.

Renner, Judith. *Discourse, Normative Change and the Quest for Reconciliation in Global Politics*. Manchester: Manchester University Press, 2013.

——. "The Local Roots of the Global Politics of Reconciliation: The Articulation of 'Reconciliation' as an Empty Universal in the South African Transition to Democracy." *Millennium: Journal of International Studies* 42, no. 2 (2014): 263–85.

Reyburn, Duncan. "Subversive Joy and Positive Reciprocity: A Chestertonian-Girardian Dialogue." *Contagion: Journal of Violence, Mimesis, and Culture* 21 (2014): 157–73.

Rieff, David. *A Bed for the Night: Humanitarianism in Crisis*. London: Vintage, 2002.

Rösch, Felix. "Pouvoir, Puissance, and Politics: Hans Morgenthau's Dualistic Concept of Power?" *Review of International Studies* 40 (2014): 349–65. doi: https://doi. org/10.1017/S0260210513000065.

——. "Realism as Social Criticism: The Thinking Partnership of Hannah Arendt and Hans Morgenthau." *International Politics* 50, no. 6 (2013): 815–29.

Rose, Gideon. "Neoclassical Realism and Theories of Foreign Policy." *World Politics* 51 (October 1998): 144–72.

Rosenau, James N. "Probing Puzzles Persistently: A Desirable but Improbable Future for IR Theory." In Smith, Booth, and Zalewski, *Positivism and Beyond*, 309–17.

Ross, Andrew A. G. *Mixed Emotions: Beyond Fear and Hatred in International Conflict*. Chicago: Chicago University Press, 2014.

——. "Realism, Emotion, and Dynamic Allegiances in Global Politics." *International Theory* 5, no. 2 (2013): 273–99.

Rotberg, Robert I., and Dennis F. Thompson, eds. *Truth V. Justice: The Morality of Truth Commissions*. Princeton, NJ: Princeton University Press, 2000.

Russel, Greg. "Hans J. Morgenthau and the National Interest." *Society in Transition* 31, no. 2 (1994): 80–84.

Sakwa, Richard. "The Cold Peace: Russo-Western Relations as a Mimetic Cold War." *Cambridge Review of International Affairs* 26, no. 1 (2013): 203–24. doi: https://doi. org/10.1080/09557571.2012.710584.

Sandal, Nukhet A., and Patrick James. "Religion and International Relations Theory: Towards a Mutual Understanding." *European Journal of International Relations* 17, no. 1 (2011): 3–25.

Sanders, Rebecca. *Plausible Legality: Legal Culture and Political Imperative in the Global War on Terror.* New York: Oxford University Press, 2018.

Sassen, Saskia. "The Global Street: Making the Political." *Globalizations* 8, no. 5 (2011): 573–79. doi: https://doi.org/10.1080/14747731.2011.622458.

———. "Urban Capabilities." *Journal of International Affairs* 65, no. 2 (2012): 85–95.

Saunders, Doug. *Arrival City: The Final Migration and Our Next World.* Toronto: Knopf Canada, 2010.

Schaap, Andrew. "Reconciliation as Ideology and Politics." *Constellations* 15, no. 2 (2008): 249–64. doi: https://doi.org/10.1111/j.1467-8675.2008.00488.x.

Schachter, Oskar. "Dag Hammarskjöld and the Relation of Law to Politics." *The American Journal of International Law* 56, no. 1 (1962): 1–8.

Scheuerman, William E. "Another Hidden Dialogue: Hans Morgenthau and Carl Schmitt." In *Carl Schmitt: The End of Law*, edited by William E. Scheuerman, 225–51. New York: Rowman & Littlefield, 1999.

———. "Carl Schmitt and Hans Morgenthau: Realism and Beyond." In Williams, *Realism Reconsidered*, 62–92.

———. *Hans Morgenthau: Realism and Beyond.* Cambridge, UK: Polity Press, 2009.

———. *The Realist Case for Global Reform.* Cambridge, UK: Polity Press, 2011.

———. "The Realist Revival in Political Philosophy, or: Why New Is Not Always Improved." *International Politics* 50, no. 6 (2013): 798–814.

———. "Was Morgenthau a Realist? Revisiting Scientific Man vs. Power Politics." *Constellations* 14, no. 4 (2007): 506–30.

Schillebeeckx, Edward, ed. *Sacramental Reconciliation.* New York: Herder and Herder, 1971.

Schmitt, Carl. *The Concept of the Political.* Chicago: University of Chicago Press, 1996.

———. *Der Begriff des Politischen.* 2nd ed. Berlin: Duncker & Humbolt, 2002.

———. *Ex Captivitate Salus: Erfahrungen aus der Zeit 1945/47.* Cologne: Greven Verlag, 1950.

Schuett, Robert. "Classical Realism, Freud and Human Nature in International Relations." *History of the Human Sciences* 23, no. 2 (2010): 21–46.

———. "Freudian Roots of Political Realism: Importance of Sigmund Freud to Hans J. Morgenthau's Theory of International Power Politics." *History of the Human Sciences* 20, no. 4 (2007): 53–78.

———. *Political Realism, Freud, and Human Nature in International Relations: The Resurrection of the Realist Man*. New York: Palgrave Macmillan, 2009.

Schwartz-Shea, Peregrine, and Dvora Yanow. *Interpretive Research Design: Concepts and Processes*. New York: Routledge, 2012.

Scott, James C. *Seeing Like a State: How Certain Schemes to Improve the Human Condition Have Failed*. New Haven, CT: Yale University Press, 1998.

Scott, Kyle. "A Girardian Critique of the Liberal Democratic Peace Theory." *Contagion: Journal of Violence, Mimesis, and Culture* 15/16 (2008–2009): 45–62.

Sending, Ole Jacob. *The Politics of Expertise: Competing for Authority in Global Governance*. Ann Arbor: University of Michigan Press, 2015.

Sending, Ole Jacob, Vincent Pouliot, and Iver B. Neumann. "Introduction." In *Diplomacy and the Making of World Politics*, edited by Ole J. Sending, Vincent Pouliot, and Iver B. Neumann, 1–28. Cambridge: Cambridge University Press, 2015.

Shaap, Andrew. *Political Reconciliation*. New York: Routledge, 2005.

Shai, Lavi. "Crimes of Action, Crimes of Thought: Arendt on Reconciliation, Forgiveness, and Judgment." In *Thinking in Dark Times: Hannah Arendt on Ethics and Politics*, edited by Roger Berkowitz, Jeffrey Katz, and Thomas Keenan, 229–34. New York: Fordham University Press, 2010.

Shapcott, Richard. "IR as Practical Philosophy: Defining a 'Classical Approach.'" *British Journal of Politics and International Relations* 6, no. 3 (2004): 271–91.

Sharp, Paul. *Diplomatic Theory of International Relations*. Cambridge: Cambridge University Press, 2009.

———. "Herbert Butterfield, the English School and the Civilizing Virtues of Diplomacy." *International Affairs* 9, no. 4 (2003): 855–78.

———. "Mullah Zaeef and Taliban Diplomacy: An English School Approach." *Review of International Studies* 29 (2003): 481–98. doi: https://doi.org/10.1017/S0260210503004819.

Sheikh, Mona Kanwal. "Appointing Evil in International Relations." *International Politics* 51, no. 4 (2014): 492–507. doi: https://doi.org/10.1017/S026021051100057X.

———. "How Does Religion Matter? Pathways to Religion in International Relations." *Review of International Studies* 38 (2012): 365–92.

Shklar, Judith Nisse. *Legalism: Law, Morals, and Political Trials*. Cambridge, MA: Harvard University Press, 1964.

Shriver, Donald W. *An Ethic for Enemies: Forgiveness in Politics*. New York: Oxford University Press, 1998.

Sikkink, Kathryn. *The Justice Cascade: How Human Rights Prosecutions Are Changing World Politics*. New York: W. W. Norton, 2011.

Smith, Steve, Ken Booth, and Marysia Zalewski, eds. *Positivism and Beyond*. Cambridge: Cambridge University Press, 1996.

Snyder, Jack L., ed. *Religion and International Relations Theory*. New York: Columbia University Press, 2011.

Snyder, Jack, and Leslie Vinjamuri. "Trials and Errors: Principle and Pragmatism in Strategies of International Justice." *International Security* 28, no. 3 (2004): 5–44. doi: https://doi.org/10.1162/016228803773100066.

Steele, Brent J. *Ontological Security in International Relations: Self-Identity and the IR State*. New York: Routledge, 2008.

Stivers, Richard. "The Festival in Light of the Theory of the Three Milieus: A Critique of Girard's Theory of Ritual Scapegoating." *Journal of the American Academy of Religion* 61, no. 3 (1993): 505–38.

Stolpe, Seven. *Dag Hammarskjöld: A Spiritual Portrait*. New York: Charles Scribner's Sons, 1966.

Stone, Ronald H. *Prophetic Realism: Beyond Militarism and Pacifism in an Age of Terror*. New York: T & T Clark, 2005.

Stork, Peter. "Human Rights: Controlling the Uncontrollable?" In *Violence, Desire, and the Sacred: Girard's Mimetic Theory Across the Disciplines*. Edited by Scott Cowdell, Chris Fleming, and Joel Hodge, 205–16. New York and London: Continuum, 2012.

Taliaferro, Jeffrey W., Steven E. Lobell, and Norrin M. Ripsman. "Introduction: Neoclassical Realism, the State, and Foreign Policy." In Lobell, Ripsman, and Taliaferro, *Neoclassical Realism, the State, and Foreign Policy*, 1–41.

Taylor, Charles. *A Secular Age*. Cambridge, MA: Belknap Press, 2007.

Teitel, Ruti G. *Humanity's Law*. Oxford: Oxford University Press, 2011.

Thomas, Scott M. "Culture, Religion and Violence: Rene Girard's Mimetic Theory." *Millennium: Journal of International Studies* 43, no. 1 (2014): 308–27.

———. *The Global Resurgence of Religion and the Transformation of International Relations: The Struggle for the Soul of the Twenty-First Century*. New York: Palgrave Macmillan, 2005.

———. "Rethinking Religious Violence: Towards a Mimetic Approach to Violence in International Relations." *Journal of International Political Theory* 11, no. 1 (2015): 61–79.

Thomas, Ward. *The Ethics of Destruction: Norms and Force in International Relations*. Ithaca, NY: Cornell University Press, 2001.

Tilly, Charles. "War Making and State Making as Organized Crime." In *Bringing the State Back In*, edited by Peter B. Evans, Dietrich Rueschemeyer and Theda Skocpol, 169–91. Cambridge: Cambridge University Press, 1985.

———. *Collective Violence*. Cambridge, New York: Cambridge University Press, 2003.

Tir, J., and P. F. Diehl. "Demographic Pressure and Interstate Conflict: Linking Population Growth and Density to Militarized Disputes and Wars, 1930–89." *Journal of Peace Research* 35, no. 3 (1998): 319–39. doi: https://doi.org/10.1177/002234339803500 3004.

Tocqueville, Alexis de. *Democracy in America*. Edited by Richard D. Heffner. New York: Mentor Books, 1956.

Toft, Monica Duffy. *Securing the Peace: The Durable Settlement of Civil Wars*. Princeton, NJ: Princeton University Press, 2010.

Toft, Monica Duffy, Daniel Philpott, and Timothy Samuel Shah. *God's Century: Resurgent Religion and Global Politics*. New York: W. W. Norton, 2011.

Trachtenberg, Marc. *The Craft of International History: A Guide to Method*. Princeton, NJ: Princeton University Press, 2006.

Troy, Jodok. *Christian Approaches to International Affairs*. New York: Palgrave Macmillan, 2012.

———. "Desire for Power or the Power of Desire? Mimetic Theory and the Heart of Twentieth-Century Realism." *Journal of International Political Theory* 11, no. 1 (2015): 26–41.

Truman, Margaret. *Where the Buck Stops: The Personal and Private Writings of Harry S. Truman*. New York: Warner Books, 1990.

Turner, S., and G. Mazur. "Morgenthau as a Weberian Methodologist." *European Journal of International Relations* 15, no. 3 (2009): 477–504. doi: https://doi.org/10.1177/1354066109338242.

Tutu, Desmond. *No Future Without Forgiveness*. New York: Image, 1999.

United Nations Chronicle. "Dag Hammarskjöld: 'Virtuoso of Multilateral Diplomacy.'" *United Nations Chronicle* 28, no. 3 (1991): 74–76.

Urdal, Henrik, and Kristian Hoelscher. "Explaining Urban Social Disorder and Violence: An Empirical Study of Event Data from Asian and Sub-Saharan African Cities." *International Interactions* 38, no. 4 (2012): 512–28.

Urquhart, Brian. *Hammarskjöld*. New York: Norton, 1994.

———. "International Peace and Security: Thoughts on the Twentieth Anniversary of Dag Hammarskjöld's Death." *Foreign Affairs* 60, no. 1 (1981): 1–16.

———. "The Secretary-General: Why Dag Hammarskjöld." In Ask and Mark-Jungkoist, *The Adventure of Peace*, 14–23.

Villa-Vicencio, Charles. *Walk with Us and Listen: Political Reconciliation in Africa.* Washington, DC: Georgetown University Press, 2009.

Voegelin, Eric. *Der Gottesmord: Zur Genese und Gestalt der modernen politischen Gnosis.* Munich: Fink, 1999.

———. *Political Religions.* Lewiston, NY: E. Mellen Press, 1986.

Volf, Miroslav. *Exclusion and Embrace: A Theological Exploration of Identity, Otherness, and Reconciliation.* Nashville, TN: Abingdon Press, 1996.

———. "Forgiveness, Reconciliation, and Justice: A Theological Contribution to a More Peaceful Social Environment." *Millennium: Journal of International Studies* 29, no. 3 (2000): 861–77. doi: https://doi.org/10.1177/03058298000290030601.

Waldheim, Kurt. "Dag Hammarskjöld and the Office of United Nations Secretary-General." In *Dag Hammarskjöld Revisited: The UN Secretary-General as a Force in World Politics,* edited by Robert S. Jordan, 15–23. Durham, NC: Carolina Academic Press, 1983.

Wallace, William. "Truth and Power, Monks and Technocrats: Theory and Practice in International Relations." *Review of International Studies* 22 (1996): 301–21.

Wallensteen, Peter. *Quality Peace: Strategic Peacebuilding and World Order.* New York: Oxford University Press, 2015.

Waltz, Kenneth. *Man, the State and War: A Theoretical Analysis.* New York: Columbia University Press, 2001.

———. "Realist Thought and Neorealist Theory." *Journal of International Affairs* 44, no. 1 (1990): 21–37.

Walzer, Michael. *Thinking Politically: Essays in Political Theory.* New Haven, CT: Yale University Press, 2007.

Weber, Max. *Wirtschaft und Gesellschaft : Grundriss der verstehenden Soziologie.* 5 ed. Edited by von Johannes Winckelmann. Tübingen: J.C.B. Mohr (Paul Siebeck), 1980. .

Wedderburn, Alister. "Tragedy, Genealogy and Theories of International Relations." *European Journal of International Relations* 3, no. 2 (2017): https://doi.org/10.1177/1354066116689131.

Wendt, Alexander. "The Agent-Structure Problem in International Relations Theory." *International Organization* 41 (1987): 335–70.

———. *Social Theory of International Politics.* Cambridge: Cambridge University Press, 1999.

———. "The State as Person in International Theory." *Review of International Studies* 30, no. 2 (2004): 289–316.

Wheeler, Nicholas. *Saving Strangers: Humanitarian Intervention in International Society.* Oxford: Oxford University Press, 2000.

Wight, Martin. *International Theory: The Three Traditions*. Leicester: Leicester University Press, 1991.

———. "Western Values in International Relations." In *Diplomatic Investigations: Essays in the Theory of International Politics*, edited by Herbert Butterfield and Martin Wight, 89–131. London: Allen & Unwin, 1966.

Williams, Michael C., ed. *Realism Reconsidered: The Legacy of Hans Morgenthau in International Relations*. Oxford: Oxford University Press, 2007.

———. "Waltz, Realism and Democracy." *International Relations* 23, no. 3 (2009): 328–40.

———. "What Is the National Interest? The Neoconservative Challenge in IR Theory." *The European Journal of International Relations* 11, no. 3 (2005): 307–37.

———. "Why Ideas Matter in International Relations: Hans Morgenthau, Classical Realism, and the Moral Construction of Power Politics." *International Organization* 58, no. 4 (2004): 633–65. doi: https://doi.org/10.1017/S0020818304040202.

Williams, Rowan. "Foreword." In *Can We Survive Our Origins? Readings in René Girard's Theory of Violence and the Sacred*, edited by Pierpaolo Antonello and Paul Gifford, xi–xvi. East Lansing: Michigan State University Press, 2015.

Wolterstorff, Nicholas. "The Place of Forgiveness in the Actions of the State." In Philpott, *The Politics of Past Evil*, 87–111.

Worth, Robert Forsyth. *A Rage for Order: The Middle East in Turmoil, from Tahrir Square to ISIS*. New York: Farrar, Straus and Giroux, 2016.

Wydra, Harald. *Politics and the Sacred*. Cambridge: Cambridge University Press, 2015.

Wydra, Harald. "Victims and New Wars." *Cambridge Review of International Affairs* 26, no. 1 (2013): 161–80. doi: https://doi.org/10.1080/09557571.2012.710581.

Zakaria, Fareed. *The Post-American World: Release 2.0*. New York: W. W. Norton, 2011.

Zalewski, Marysia. "'All These Theories yet the Bodies Keep Piling Up': Theory, Theorists, Theorising." In Smith, Booth, and Zalewski, *Positivism and Beyond*, edited by Smith, Booth, and Zalewski, 340–53.

Index

Original Sin, 53
Other, the, 51–54, 58, 68

P

Pacem in Terris (Pope John XXIII), 47
Paris, France, 65–66
peacekeeping, term, 99 (n. 47)
Philpott, Daniel, 29, 30–31
Plato, 12
political individualization, 61–63
political reconciliation. *See* reconciliation
political theory vs. political practice, 5–7, 11,
    17, 58, 66
Politics among Nations (Morgenthau), 7, 24
positivism, 17
power, 6–7, 21–23. *See also* desire; imitation;
    mimetic theory
practical knowledge, xv
practice: in international politics, 5–7, 11, 17,
    58; in science, 7–8

Q

Qatar, 61

R

rationalism: of Aron, 20; of Morgenthau,
    17, 20–21; on norms and ideas, 3;
    Oakshott on, xv
Ratzinger, Cardinal. *See* Benedict XVI
    (pope)
Realism, 1–2, 17, 67–69; mimetic theory
    and, xvii–xx, 17–23, 27–28; power and,
    6, 25–27; on reconciliation, 30, 34. *See
    also* Morgenthau, Hans J.
realistic optimism, 42–46, 51, 68
reciprocity, 37, 67
recognition and identity politics, 13–14,
    59–61, 72 (n. 3)
reconciliation, 29–31; mimetic theory and,
    35–39; political quality of, 33–35. *See
    also* justice
religious ideas and symbols: Juergensmeyer
    on, 16; Kantorowitcz on, 75 (n. 44);
    mimetic theory on, xix, 12–13, 15–17;
    terrorism and, 4; of UN, 47–49. *See*

also Christianity; Islam; Judaism
reparations, 31
repentance, 31
resentment, globalization of, 64–65
responsibility, 31, 62, 67
rivalry. *See* mimetic rivalry
Russia, 60, 61
Rwandan genocide, 13–14, 31, 34, 35

S

sacrificial ritual, xiv
Sassen, Saskia, 65
scapegoat mechanism, xix, 12, 14–17, 26–27,
    62, 69. *See also* mimetic theory
Schmitt, Carl, 22, 23, 26, 32, 33
Schweitzer, Albert, 43
Science: Servant or Master (Morgenthau), 25
Scientific Man vs. Power Politics
    (Morgenthau), 20–21
Scott, James, 65
Secular Age, A (Taylor), 19
self-preservation, 6, 25–26
Sharp, Paul, 47
"Significance of Being Alone, The"
    (Morgenthau), 25
skepticism, 11, 17, 24
Smith, Steve, xvii
social cohesion, 29
social justice. *See* justice
South Africa, 29–33, 59
spiritual goods and peace, 16–17, 85 (n. 45)
Steele, Brent, 18
structural violence. *See* violence
Suez Canal crisis (1956), 46, 50, 99 (n. 47)
summum bonum, 13
Syria, 61, 63

T

Taliban, 61
Talking to the Enemy (Atran), 37, 58
Taylor, Charles, 19
technical knowledge, xv
terrorism, 4, 62, 67, 107 (n. 73)
Thatcher, Margaret, 63
Tilly, Charles, 4